AGAINST JOHN HICK:

AN EXAMINATION OF HIS PHILOSOPHY OF RELIGION

Terry Richard Mathis

UNIVERSITY
PRESS OF
AMERICA

240236

LANHAM • NEW YORK • LONDON

All University Press of America books are produced on acid-free
paper which exceeds the minimum standards set by the National
Historical Publications and Records Commission.

For my wife, Laura,
and my parents,
without whose love and support
this essay could not have been written

ACKNOWLEDGEMENTS

I am grateful to Stephen T. Davis, John K. Roth, and Alfred R. Louch for their critical interaction with the manuscript as it was being written as a dissertation for Claremont Graduate School. Professor Davis has since read and helpfully commented upon a final draft of the conclusion. Charles M. Young of Claremont Graduate School should be mentioned for his role in setting the tone of the first two chapters. Though the title *Against John Hick* is to the point, it is not meant to convey animosity. I am indebted to Professor Hick for his willingness to let me undertake this project while a student in philosophy at Claremont, where he is the head of the Religion Department.

Several others I should thank for their part in helping me prepare the manuscript for publication are Ruth Baldwin, Deborah Krois, Ann Wat, Irene Reed, Janet Gathright, Laura Palmberg, Gaynia Menninger, Denise Adams, and Lloyd Richey.

TABLE OF CONTENTS

PREFACE

The aim of this study is to examine and critically evaluate the philosophy of religion of John Hick. I refer to his having a philosophy of religion in the sense that he advocates a method of philosophical inquiry and consequently an understanding of religious phenomena that he takes to be integral to his own unique philosophical theology. In order to evaluate his views in their context, the first three chapters provide an introduction both to his overall position and to the contemporary issues with which he deals. Thereafter I proceed with my criticisms, finding most importantly that he does not have sufficient justification for the kind of theistic claims he wants to make. I reach this conclusion by playing him against his own empirical orientation to matters of fact, and since the veracity of his account of this empiricist linguistic framework is assumed, my evaluation of his work is carried on internally. My criticisms generally depend upon a lack of consistency and coherence within Hick's system of thought itself. Little attention is given to the strengths and liabilities of any particular philosophical or theological orientation he may adopt. My strategy is to assume the legitimacy of these orientations in the manner they happen to be construed by his system. In doing so, I find that he attempts to build upon a secular empiricist base that excludes the possibility of the theological superstructure he hopes to erect.

CHAPTER I

INTRODUCTION

John Hick[1] is recognized as one of the foremost contemporary philosophers of religion in the Western tradition. The extent of his work and the clarity with which he has handled some of the most complex problems of religious philosophy are rarely surpassed. Prominent among his many works and acclaimed as a modern theological classic is his book, *Evil and the God of Love*, first published in 1966. His other works also continue to have a significant impact. These include *Faith and Knowledge* (1957), *Philosophy of Religion* (1963), *Faith and the Philosophers* (edited, 1964), *Classical and Contemporary Readings in the Philosophy of Religion* (ed., 1964), *The Existence of God* (ed., 1964), *The Many-faced Argument* (ed. with Arthur C. McGill, 1967), *The Center of Christianity* (1968), *Arguments for the Existence of God* (1971), *Biology and the Soul* (1972), *God and the Universe of Faiths* (1973), *Truth and Dialogue* (ed., 1974), *Death and Eternal Life* (1976), *The Myth of God Incarnate* (ed., 1977), *Christianity and Other Religions* (ed. with Brian Hebblethwaite, 1980), and *God Has Many Names* (1980). His articles and reviews are too numerous to mention here.

Although Hick shows sensitivity for and is indebted to the historical circumstances and the various traditions associated with religious thought, he has his own unique philosophical theology which I will refer to as his system of thought. Broad as it is, Hick's thought, taken as a whole, constitutes a sustained defense of a theistic understanding of the universe. Among those parts of his system that can be distinguished, such as his theodicy, soteriology, theory of knowledge, and so

1

forth, there is a varying degree of interdependence, so that criticism of the more crucial parts of his thought may well affect his entire system.

The aspects of his thinking that this study will focus upon have mainly to do with his means of dealing with assertions that are supposed to entail knowledge and experience of God.[2] Since the possibility of the truth of such assertions is related foundationally to his entire system of thought, this study will come into contact with most of the major segments of Hick's thinking. To show the purpose of this study more specifically, I will first set forth some of the details of his thought.

Hick is attempting to develop a global, pluralistic, philosophical theology in which some of the major world religions are understood to be variously related to the same divine reality. To do this, he is comparing those religious or theological affirmations of the different world faiths that he believes are capable of some degree of empirical verification.[3] Hick is well aware that religious assertions raise special problems in this regard, since they typically make reference to supernatural beings and their places of habitation. He realizes also that the experiences he thinks would confirm theological assertions are not reported by many people. Hick nevertheless believes that everyone eventually will come to have a post-mortem awareness of a divine reality, an awareness which will verify at least some religious assertions. The possibility that these propositions will in this way be verified shows them, in Hick's view, to be factual in nature, and because their verification will occur after this life, he describes their mode of verification as eschatological. For Hick, then, the notion that certain theological propositions are eschatologically verifiable gives them factual status and makes possible meaningful comparisons across religious traditions.

This notion of eschatological verification provides the focus for my study of Hick's work. I will try to show that his verificationist approach to religious questions does not need to include eschatological verification. Contrary to what Hick thinks, this notion will be found to be unnecessary. I will argue that, if one accepts Hick's own account of the nature of religious experience, his description of the verifying experience entails that its conditions could obtain in this life. Talk about God could thus be considered factual in nature without appeal to eschatological verification.

My focus upon the notion of eschatological verification will indicate, however, that this notion is dependent upon his account of religious experience. Accordingly, after raising several criticisms to which his account of religious experience is vulnerable, we will find that he neither has reason to make eschatological hypotheses nor sufficient foundation for most of the other religious parts of his system. His approach will be found to be without an adequate factual basis.

In the present chapter, which lays the ground for the main work of this study, I provide a synopsis of several philosophical themes that have influenced both Hick's understanding of experience of God and his attempt to use the possibility of such experience to show religious talk to be verifiable. I will not criticize Hick in this chapter, but the discussion of philosophical influences will put us in a position to consider the nature of the criticisms to which we will proceed in the chapters that follow. Also in the present chapter, finally, I will provide a summary of primary elements of Hick's theology to which I will later refer.

1. The Issue in Its Philosophical Setting

Hick believes that the central problem any theology such as his must face is whether or not its assertions are empirically confirmable. His concern with this problem is largely the result of his view of the relationship of experience to factual assertions. He thinks that a factual statement about experiential objects and situations is true if the state of affairs to which it refers can be experienced to exist independently of our thoughts about it. Conversely, a statement is thought to be false if its purported facts cannot possibly be obtained. Language that is factual in that it asserts the reality of a possible but not necessarily actual state of affairs in the universe is referred to as cognitive, whereas language that cannot be used to affirm the possibility of some such objective state of affairs is said to be noncognitive. Religious utterances, in Hick's view, may accordingly be instances of either the cognitive or the noncognitive uses cf language.[4] How it is that talk about God can thus be thought to be cognitive will be seen later. Assuming it can be, cognitive religious language is supposed to assert facts while noncognitive religious utterances only express the believer's subjective mental state. While Hick thinks it appropriate for people to express their religious feelings, if a religious utterance does not convey information that is capable of being true or false, Hick calls it noncognitive.

But threatening Hick's view are several theories that have it that all religious language is noncognitive. These will be considered in chapter II. What is usually common among them is that they explicate the function of religious language as primarily a product of the psychological needs of the language user. Religious language is thought to function to vent a speaker's emotional state and perhaps sometimes to induce this state in others. A religious person's feelings of remorse expressed through penitent language might, for example, indicate a state of depression and self-criticism, while language of thanksgiving to God might symbolize feelings of euphoria. Or religious language may signify awe-inspiring aspects of the world which evoke in the mind various feelings about life's cosmic dependence or the valued of community, posterity, morality, and the like. But when religious utterances are taken literally as referring to an unobservable, transcendent entity called God, they are, according to the noncognitivist view, cognitively meaningless.

One central problem of theology is thus to find a means to combat noncognitivist theories. It must be shown, thinks Hick, that some religious utterances are in principle verifiable in that they may correspond to an actual state of affairs that can be experienced independently of an individual's mental state. Hick is not suggesting that religious statements must be verified, but that they be verifiable in principle. This means that the person using religious language should at least be capable of specifying what would count as a confirming experience of the language used, even though a full-fledged experience of this sort may never have been reported. Hick has in this way distinguished between verifiability and verification. Talk about water underneath an unexplored, ice-covered area of the Antarctic continent is, for instance, cognitive, because conceivably one can travel to the area with the proper equipment and check. Likewise, Hick seems to think Muhammad spoke cognitively about a heavenly existence after death, for if a person survives death, this person's experience may then confirm the teaching of the Koran. This person's experience might also, however, disconfirm Muhammad's claims. Language that is cognitive, because it is verifiable, may turn out to be false. Only after a statement has been verified does it carry the distinction of being known to be true.[5]

In order to be cognitive, then, Hick thinks that some religious language must in principle be capable of experiential verification. If it is not, Hick foresees that the faith embodied in religious writings and the faith of many people that extends from these writings will be lost. For implicit in the use of a great deal of religious language is the requirement that it should function cognitively. Statements such as "God created the heavens and the earth" or "God is a very present help in time of need" or "Shiva is the energy of life" or "Muhammad is the prophet of Allah" are presumably each intended by the typical user either to presuppose (in the case of prayer) or entail (in the course of ordinary discussion) the extralinguistic reality of a divine being.[6] What is meant in normal use of these religious statements is therefore quite different from what is advanced by the noncognitivist theories. According to the noncognitivist view, even if these utterances fulfill the purposes that the noncognitivists claim they fulfill, there need be no God to which they refer. And if the noncognitivist view is correct, Hick thinks the religious apologist would then have no cause to argue such things as that life on earth exists according to the will and the purpose of an infinite creative mind.[7] So the survival of historic religious traditions depends upon the possibility of some

5

religious language being cognitive. Noncognitive theories would not, in Hick's opinion, instigate an enlightened revision of religious traditions; these theories would spell the obituary of religion.[8]

We find, then, that theology's central problem, as Hick sees it, is to show that religious utterances are in some instances true or false factual assertions. His means of dealing with this problem most notably reflect the influence of Immanuel Kant and the logical positivists. The nature of the problem, as well as Hick's attempt to deal with it, will perhaps be better seen in light of a brief recounting of these two sources of influence. We will begin with Kant.

In his *Critique of Pure Reason*, Kant intended to bring together two epistemological extremes. Kant believed that although all our knowledge begins with experience, the mind also plays an essential role. There is in Kant thus both an empiricist and a rationalist element. The former is seen in his belief that perception depends upon sense experiences of things in themselves; whatever objects are out there in the world evoke in us manifold sensations. So experience is a primary source of knowledge. But together with experience is a rationalist emphasis upon an ability of the mind to structure what appears to one's consciousness. Kant thought that what orders an appearance and gives it its form are the several functions of the intellect that mold and shape sensual input and thus bring about what is finally called knowledge. Since this knowledge is of sensation, not things in themselves, the objects of knowledge are limited to the mental realm.[9]

Kant entitles such objects of appearance "phenomena." While phenomena have to do with the mode of consciousness in which we intuit things, in contrast, what he calls "noumena" have to do with things as they are in themselves. The noumena are not objects of our senses, but are thought of as objects or intelligible entities by an operation of the mind. Kant thought that a noumenal reality is a domain into which the understanding cannot go. The mind is insulated by its field of sensibility from actual contact with the noumenal realm. The concept of a noumenal realm is merely postulated as an extension or dimension beyond the appearances of sensation in order to explain what gives rise to sensation.

Hick says that he is not at all concerned with the assessment of Kant's philosophy.[10] Kant's positive contribution, according to Hick, is that the modern world was enabled to recognize that the mind furnishes its own recognitional capacities to the perceived character of the physical environment. But aside from this contribution, Hick intends only to borrow an aspect of Kant's system to use in the sphere of the epistemology of religion to account for the various claims of experience of God. Hick acknowledges that Kant would not have sanctioned any attempt to account for experience of God, because Kant did not think it was possible.[11] Hick nevertheless suggests that a person can experience a divine reality and that when that happens, something occurs to which Kant's distinction between noumena and phenomena is highly relevant. Hick thinks that God should "...be thought of as the divine noumenon, experienced by mankind as a range of divine phenomena which take both theistic and non-theistic forms."[12] Which form it takes depends upon variations in the social-cultural situation and one's human spiritual capacities. The particular image of God that informs a person's religious awareness might then be that of Allah, Vishnu, Shiva, or the God of Israel, or whatever.[13]

Hick believes that awareness of God (the difference that is made by an experience of God) is somewhat like that awareness which is derived through sensation. Just as we do not experience things in themselves, but only sensations of things, Hick thinks we never actually experience God, but only a significance that is distinct from the divine noumenon. Religious significance is thought to be related to a divine noumenal reality in much the same way as ordinary experience of sensations is related to a physical reality.[14] It is thus an awareness of religious significance that amounts to experience of God. This religious awareness is thought in some cases to be a supplemental interpretation or a higher level of awareness of the material en-

7

vironment, though it may also be a mystical awareness apart from ordinary experience. Hick believes one may contemplate God relatively independently of objective circumstances external to the mind, perhaps while the mind is engrossed in prayer or meditation. In either event, whether with or without external circumstances, it is experience of God that substantiates thinking and talking about God for Hick.[15]

Such a religious experience is understood to be similar to ordinary experience as it includes what Hick calls experiencing-as.[16] This is the proposal that all experience of sense data carries a significance that is derived through an interpretation of these data, which significance both varies with and is dependent upon one's perceptual capacity and one's cultural situation. What one person sees as an easily held, smooth oblong stone may for another person (an Indian) appear to be a tool for grinding corn. Or what would to many people appear to be simply a dial on an electronic device could be recognized by a physicist as an indication of negative ions. Similarly, according to Hick, we may experience the events of our lives and of human history as either purely natural events or as mediating the presence and activity of God. The Hebrew prophets are examples of people who were capable of the latter. Hick says that when the Chaldeans were at the gates of Jerusalem, the prophet Jeremiah experienced this event (was aware of its significance) not only as a foreign political threat, but also as the judgment of God upon Israel. Behind and through the serried ranks of the Chaldean army, Hick suggests that Jeremiah was able to sense the form of God fighting against Israel.[17] Yet in Hick's view, Jeremiah may have also been able to interpret these events naturalistically. The objects and events of the material environment are believed to be religiously ambiguous.

Whether experience carries the significance of naturalism or theism, in either case there is thought to be an interpretation of objects and situations that is not provided in the data of experience itself. All conscious perceiving is thought to include an awareness of significance that goes beyond what the senses report. Phenomena such as table

8

lamps and football games are recognized or identified by way of concepts that are social products developed within a specific social environment, as Hick thinks is also true of what some people express about their perceived image of God. As people learn to identify the natural environment with one type of significance or another, so, too, Hick believes that people are also capable of learning to identify the world in relation to God.[18] Hick thinks this awareness of God that may supplement ordinary experience may be as vivid and forceful as one's ordinary experience of the material environment.

It is this sort of vivid awareness of God that Hick thinks will provide eschatological verification of the theistic interpretation of the universe. We will discuss this possibility in more detail in chapters III through V. Hick believes that when people experience God this forcefully, it is then rational for them to talk and live in terms of this experience, for the religious awareness in such cases (those of the great religious leaders such as the prophets and gurus) is supposedly as real as ordinary experience of the world.

Verification of the theistic interpretation of the universe might thus be realized presently for some individuals, in Hick's way of thinking, were it not for the disconfirming experiences of pain and suffering in this world. Evil circumstances involving suffering may cause people to doubt whether there is a perfectly good, unlimitedly powerful God who is directing the course of the universe, for according to Hick, people often think that a good, omniscient God would abolish the world's evils if this God were truly omnipotent.[19] Hick predicts that the eschatological situation, however, will not include the disconfirming evil circumstances of the present world, so that the theistic account of the universe can then be verified.

Many of the objections to what Hick is proposing have been drawn from logical positivism.[20] The positivists tried to devise a criterion by which to distinguish language of fact (language that can be empirically verified), from other types of language they believed to be nonfactual. The issues involved in their attempt to do this have often been

9

central in contemporary philosophy of religion and thus have also been a basic influence upon the development of Hick's system of thought. Hick has attempted to accommodate the positivist contention that factual language must be verifiable.[21]

The positivists generally believed that only two kinds of statements are meaningful. These were classified as either analytic or synthetic. Analytic statements were recognized to range in complexity from the equations of higher mathematics and logic to fairly trivial statements, such as "All red objects are red," which despite their degree of complexity are necessarily true, their denial always a contradiction. Without any reference to experience of the world, their character is determined by the meaning of their terms and the logical rules that govern the use of these terms. So although they are not factually informative of states of affairs in the world, they were seen to be important as they provide information about the logical structure of a system of thought.

Synthetic statements were seen much differently. They were understood to be factually informative in that they may convey information about some specific state of affairs or object of the world. Such statements are therefore not necessarily true. Their truth or falsity is determined by observing via the senses (primarily sight, hearing, and touch) that object or situation to which they refer. They are statements like, "John Hick is a professor at Claremont," which are capable of empirical verification.

The positivist movement became most threatening to theism as it was marshaled by A. J. Ayer in his book, *Language, Truth and Logic*, published initially in 1936. Of the two kinds of propositions that were understood to be meaningful, propositions about God would fit into neither category. One might say that "God is omnipotent" or that "God is good" or that "God necessarily exists," intending that the attributes of omnipotence, goodness, and necessary existence define in each statement what is meant by the term "God." As tautologous utterances, they would be true because of the meaning of their terms. But they would in no way establish that there

10

really is a God whose attributes are infinite, only that if there is a God so described, this God must have such attributes. If, on the other hand, these statements are meant to be synthetic, Ayer did not think they could be verified by experience. Empirical theological statements are not possible, because, according to Ayer, an infinite God cannot be a tangible aspect of one's perception. It cannot be said that God is known through some sort of empirical manifestation, because God is thought to transcend any empirical situation. Ayer believed that an empirical manifestation should always simply be understood as such, for he thought, and probably still thinks, that an empirical situation does not provide evidence for anything other than a natural state of affairs.[22]

But Ayer's verification criteria proved to be too restrictive, for they denied the status of factual meaning to many statements that the positivists themselves thought were noncontroversial, such as the universal laws and generalizations of the sciences. The core of the positivist tradition to which Hick is indebted has accordingly undergone some moderation since Ayer's day. Hick states that Herbert Feigl's suggestion of confirmability-in-principle, in contrast to early positivist views, is modest and entirely acceptable.[23] Feigl is suggesting that the requirement of verification (as well as the falsification criterion that was later developed to take the place of verification) should be replaced with a test of confirmation.[24] That is, it must be possible to specify observations that would in principle count as evidence either for or against the truth of a proposition. Specifying such evidence is not thought to count conclusively for the truth of a proposition; it only counts partially, and therefore the term "confirmation" is used rather than "verification." With regard to terms used to refer to unobservable theoretical entities such as photons or neutrinos, Feigl suggests that they should at least logically connect with terms of an appropriate observation base of empirical concepts that are derived from experience of the material environment.[25] In Feigl's view, experience is the soil of observation from which "...there is an 'upward seepage' of meaning from the observational terms to the theoretical concepts."[26]

In aligning himself with Feigl's suggestion of confirm-ability-in-principle, Hick seems to imply that he prefers some formulations of confirmation theory over others. Perhaps so, but for the purpose of this study, the point of interest need only be with the requirements of confirmation that Hick himself specifies. There are many undecided issues in current philosophical discussion of confirmation theory,[27] but I shall assume that the view of confirmation explicit in Hick's published material is adequate and normative for the evaluation of religious utterances. Though on occasion I will question Hick's view of confirmation, to do much of this would lead us away from the internal workings of his thinking and into the issues of probability theory and induction.

I will usually refer to Hick's view of confirmation in terms of verification, as I have done all along, because he construes the notion of confirmation so as to allow for verification of theistic assertions. The concepts of confirmation and verification coincide, according to Hick, at the point of cognitive conclusiveness. This is the point at which confirmation has become so strong that a rational observer can no longer doubt the truth of the proposition in question, and it may even be reached with large-scale scientific hypotheses. He says that in cases such as the theory of evolution, "...there may be increasing confirmation until the point of cognitive conclusiveness is reached."[28] Hick thus seems to be a bit more optimistic than Feigl. Whether or not Hick is overly ambitious will not be of much concern to us except as his views have to do with religious propositions.

What must happen to exclude rational doubt may in any event (whether scientific or religious) be no simple matter, as we shall see in chapter III. Hick generally supposes, as we have seen, that it happens when an individual has a vivid experience of the state of affairs to which the proposition in question refers, there being no significant experience to the contrary that would disconfirm the truth of this proposition. Though the conditions required to confirm some propositions may not obtain, as long as they can be predicted, Hick believes this proposition should be considered factual.

Hick thinks that when a statement predicts the state of affairs by which it can be found to be true or false, its character as a cognitive assertion (though not necessarily its truth) is thereby guaranteed.[29] Many religious propositions are therefore thought to have cognitive status because they predict a state of affairs, the experience of which would exclude grounds for rational doubt of their truth.

Though many people do not currently experience the states of affairs that would verify religious statements, propositions such as "there will be a post-mortem awareness of the divine reality" have cognitive status in Hick's view, because they predict conditions that may eventually be verified.[30] Hick in fact maintains that there will be an eschatological situation in which we shall fully experience the presence and loving purpose of an infinite being, and it is the possibility of the experience of this situation, predicted by Hick's theology, that he thinks provides its crucial propositions about afterlife with cognitive or factual status.[31] What is predicted could be proved false if the eschatological situation turned out to be other than what was predicted. Hick's assertion that the end-state of the universe will include universal human awareness of a benevolent God would be false, for example, if the universe proved to be forever dominated by an evil power. If, however, we perish totally at death, predictions of post-mortem religious experience would not be shown false unless it could be proved that we totally perish at death.[32] Not believing we will perish, Hick predicts that his description of ordinary experience that we saw earlier in terms of experiencing-as will in the future also describe the nature or character of one's eschatological experience. Consciousness of God will continue to involve an activity of interpretation, but Hick thinks the data will then be unambiguous enough that everyone will be fully aware of God.[33]

Other philosophers of religion in the empiricist tradition have attempted to use some version of eschatological verification either to establish or criticize one theological point or another.[34] But our interest will remain with Hick's use of this notion. To re-emphasize my thesis, we will find that eschatological verification is not needed in Hick's system of thought.

Religious assertions, I shall argue, should be thought by Hick to be factual as the result of the possibility of verification in this life. If such verification is not possible, conversely, we will find that it is implausible for Hick to think that a proposed eschatological situation should be any different.

After a summary of the highlights of Hick's theology in the remaining introductory remarks, in chapter II, I will cope with several issues that might undercut my thesis. They imply that eschatological verification is unnecessary for reasons other than those I will advance. In chapter III, I will develop a more detailed account of what it is in Hick's view that makes an assertion factual and how eschatological verification is thought to meet these requirements. In chapter IV, I will then try to show that eschatological verification is unnecessary in Hick's system of thought, in that the conditions that supposedly provide factual assertion status for the religious assertions in question may be fulfilled here and now. First we will see that Hick's arguments in support of the supposed religious ambiguity of the material environment do not work, thus opening the possibility that those who claim there is evidence for theism are correct. Next we will see that, given Hick's account of religious experience, it is plausible that anyone could, in principle, experience the world's evils as compatible with the presence and purpose of a loving God. But in chapter V, we will find that Hick's understanding of religious experience is questionable as a basis for cognitive religious claims, and that unless he can deal with various weaknesses in his thinking, he has little ground for even predicting an eschatological situation. Chapter VI will then briefly assess the impact of this study upon Hick's system of thought.

A synopsis of that part of Hick's theology with which we shall be concerned is developed, again without criticism, in what follows.

2. The Theological Setting

Philosophy of religion is, according to Hick, a second-order activity that is removed from its subject matter. It is philosophical thinking about religion. He says that the "...atheist, the agnostic, and the man of faith all can and do philosophize about religion. Philosophy of religion is, accordingly, not a branch of theology (meaning by 'theology' the systematic formulation of religious beliefs), but a branch of philosophy."[35] While Hick himself is thus by his own account primarily a philosopher of religion, he is nevertheless also a theologian as he is involved in both an ongoing reformulation of the Christian tradition and the construction of a global theology. This theology is not a dogmatic systemization that cannot be altered.[36] Its conclusions are like hypotheses that are open to revision as new situations develop, two factors being of major concern. These are the developments of modern science and increasing means of worldwide communication by which the various different religions are being brought into contact.

It is the influence of science, says Hick, that has made much of the content of traditional Christian belief incredible. Beliefs about the origin of the universe, that man was created perfect but fell through his own wrong choice into sin and misery, that God intervenes in history by miraculous happenings, that God became incarnate in Christ to atone for human sin and was resurrected after his death, that heaven or hell awaits a person after death, that a divinely inspired record of all of this can be found in Scripture, and other such mythical concepts of a pre-scientific culture, are quite untenable or open to serious doubt, in Hick's view.[37] Yet he thinks that the fact of God's existence will increasingly be recognized throughout the world.

Despite the seemingly incongruent conceptions of God often reported by adherents of the various non-Christian world religions, Hick believes that as worldwide communication continues, people will become aware that the God of Christianity is the same ontological reality to which many of the other major religions besides Christianity are related. We have seen that there are various conceptions of God, the differences of which are thought to be due to both environmental circumstances and human perception. In each case, the same divine reality is believed to be self-revealingly active towards mankind with a single purpose. God wants us to be

15

less selfish. The egocentricity that was required for the initial phase of the emergence and preservation of life should now be overcome. So the challenge addressed to us by each of the great religions in the current phase of human history is for voluntary transcendence of egotism.[38] It is possible, as was true of the man Jesus, to become a less egotistical, more God-conscious person.

This pluralistic global theology is intentionally developed upon a secular base. Hick thinks there can in principle be "...a complete and consistent non-religious understanding of the universe."[39] Unbounded by both space and time, the universe can be understood to have had no initial state, and therefore it can be explained without reference to a prior divine creative reality. Its formation is intelligible to us by way of the basic laws exhibited in the behavior of matter, and the origin of life is likewise intelligible through the self-ordering of molecules to form polymers of amino acids as the building blocks of primitive proteins.[40] The development of life in response to the environment can be understood by means of the mechanism of genetic mutations and self-copying, our own minds being the most complex development of the universe now known to us.

Given this description of the emergence of man through the various forms of life, Hick believes that it is possible

> ...to understand man's moral and religious experience and beliefs as functional responses to the pressures of his situation as a gregarious animal whose intelligence is able to generate concepts not directly tied to his sense experience. Morality has developed as the method of self-regulation which makes social existence possible; and religion has developed as an outlet for our more fundamental anxieties and wishes, fulfilling a function parallel to but more basic than that of our nightly dreams: in his religions man is day-dreaming.[41]

Hick concludes that, in broad principle, the entire phenomenon of human life and experience, and the physical universe from "...which it has emerged, are intelligible in exlusively nonreligious terms."[42] Though there are gaps in the descriptive theories of science that must yet be filled before a fully convincing causal web of explanation will have been produced, we should assume this work will be done, thinks Hick, so that theologians must develop a theological picture that will stand up after it has been accomplished.

Hick's sketch of this picture, as the foregoing illustrates, has two prominent components.[43] One is naturalism, or humanism as it is referred to, and the other is the plurality of religions. These are opposed to each other if the naturalist component includes the assumption that there is no God, for this assumption would undermine what most religious people think is the basis of their religious convictions. But Hick does not think this assumption should be included in the theoretical possibility of a unified scientific description of the universe.[44] Though scientists have no reason to refer to God in order to explain the workings of nature, Hick believes their descriptions of nature do not require the explicit denial of God's existence. As long as science does not assume an atheistic stance, Hick believes its hypotheses are compatible with a conception of God such as that affirmed in his own global theology. Hick's theological picture is thus meant to augment a scientific account of the universe as described by his doctrine of experiencing-as mentioned earlier. The relationship between a scientific and a religious account of the world is such that though any event is presumably completely explicable in exclusively naturalistic scientific terms, some people may yet perceive the world religiously. That some people do not respond toward the world religiously while others do, and that different individuals in a group at the same time and in the same place may experience the world both religiously and nonreligiously, indicates to Hick, as we have seen, that the world is religiously ambiguous.[45]

That the world is religiously ambiguous or that the physical universe has an autonomous character that invites an account that is comprehensive and nonreligious is of its own theological significance,

> ...for any development of scientific knowledge, describing the natural order more and more fully without reference to God is compatible with the hypothesis that he has deliberately created a universe in which he is not compulsorily evident but is known

17

only by a free personal response of faith.[46]

The religious amibiguity of the world allows people to be cognitively free in relation to God, so that the possibility of coming to know God depends upon an uncompelled response. One's initial awareness of God is not as vivid and inescapable as one's awareness of the physical world, because a compelled experience of the Supreme Being would destroy our freedom as moral agents, and the end for which God has created people requires that they be cognitively free in relation to value-laden aspects of reality. The world must therefore be religiously ambiguous if God is to realize the end for which people were created.

As this end includes overcoming egotism, it is enhanced by an awareness of God, because people then realize that they are in God's care and that they do not need constantly to safeguard their own interests over against those of others.[47] Through fellowship with God, people will realize too that there is a divine ordering of the universe or a patterning that constitutes the Christian ethic to which they will adhere, since they will be disposed to act in accord with their beliefs.[48]

Overcoming egotism is thought further to necessitate the circumstances of evil and suffering in the world for which God is ultimately responsible.[49] The world provides an environment that is intended to make possible the growth of the finest characteristics of personal life in free beings. It must operate according to dependable laws, and it must involve real difficulties, obstacles, dangers, and possibilities of sorrow, frustration, and failure if there are to be moral values and free moral choice. These difficulties that enable human growth have been encountered through two different developmental stages. Through the first stage of biological evolution

> ...man has been made as a person in the image of God but has not yet been brought as a free and responsible agent into the finite likeness of God, which is revealed in Christ. Our world, with all its rough edges, is the sphere in which this second and harder stage of the creative process is taking place.[50]

The natural order is built not so much to comfort as to challenge us, not as punishment for sin but as a divinely appointed situation in which personal maturation and moral responsibility are possible.

That the world is designed for the purpose of soul making is thought to point forward in two ways to life after death. First, though good is often brought out of evil by a person's appropriate response to it, sometimes evil causes the disintegration and breakdown of character. Hick reasons, therefore, that any divine purpose of soul making that is currently at work in earthly history must continue far beyond this life if it is ever to achieve even a very partial and fragmentary success.[51] The disparity between our present state and our eventual perfection is so great that our eventual perfection must require the equivalent of many earthly lives, perhaps on the order of tens of hundreds.[52] Second, if one asks whether God's purpose in soul making is worth all the toil and sorrow of human life, Hick's answer is that there will finally be a future good that is great enough to justify all that was required for its realization.[53]

Hick hypothesizes that it is during the period between an individual's series of lives that a considerable degree of person-making will occur. Hick believes that the transition from one life to the next will be through

> ...a temporary *bardo phase* in which the disembodied consciousness, creating its own mind-dependent world, and finding its real desires reflected in that world, comes to a greater self-knowledge. This is a kind of psycho-analytic experience, preparing the individual for a relative new beginning. Thus the further lives are not mere quantitative continuations of the present life, but part of a spiritual progress towards the ultimate state which lies beyond the series of finite lives.[54]

One might suspect that the final eschatological state will never be reached by those individuals who do not choose to be conscious of the presence and purpose of God. Hick, however, believes that the future good of the eschaton is an end-state that everyone will realize sooner or later. Eons might pass before some of us make it, but we all will, and this prediction of universal salvation further emphasizes how Hick is using the term "freedom" and what he means by "soul making."

"God does not have to coerce us to respond to him," says Hick, "for he has already so created us that our nature, seeking its own fulfillment and good, leads us to him."[55] Hick believes that God's "...purpose for us is so indelibly written into our nature that the fulfillment of this purpose is the basic condition of our own personal self-fulfillment and happiness."[56] We are free, then, insofar as we can do whatever we want, our activities being limited by the bounds of what we as created beings cannot do. We cannot breathe, for example, without oxygen, and we need a certain amount of food, sleep, exercise, and so on. But within these bounds we are thought to experience greater utility in choosing to be conscious of God's presence and purpose. We are free to do what gives rise to pain, but we naturally pursue well-being, and this leads us, Hick believes, to God. The sense in which we are free is thus understood to be compatible with the circumstances by which God subtly directs the process of the making of our souls. God does his part and we supposedly will eventually realize that through his leading we have chosen to accommodate his purpose for our lives.

We have now a summary of some of the major components of Hick's theology. In the chapters that follow, we will see how well they fare in light of Hick's criteria for what count as matters of fact.

NOTES

[1]John Harwood Hick grew up in the Anglican church. He was converted to evangelical Christianity at age eighteen while a law student at University College, Hull. Shortly thereafter he joined the Presbyterian Church of England and went to Edinburgh intending eventually to enter the ministry. After working in the Friends' Ambulance Unit during the

war and returning to Edinburgh to take an M.A. with honors in philosophy, Hick continued his education at Oriel College, Oxford, where he earned the D.Phil. in 1950. He received further training at Westminster Theological College, Cambridge, and then served as minister of the Belford Presbyterian Church, Northumberland, until taking the position of Assistant Professor of Philosophy at Cornell University (1956-1959) and later Stuart Professor of Christian Philosophy at Princeton Theological Seminary (1959-1964) and later still Lecturer in the Philosophy of Religion at Cambridge University, there receiving a Ph.D. by incorporation in 1964. In 1967 he was appointed the H. G. Wood Professor of Theology at the University of Birmingham, and while holding this position obtained the D. Litt. from Edinburgh, awarded in 1974. He has also been a guest lecturer in numerous universities throughout the world and in 1977 was given an honorary doctorate in theology by Uppsala in Sweden. Currently, he is residing in California for much of the school year as the Danforth Professor of Religion at Claremont Graduate School.

The extent of Hick's publications is impressive (see bibliography). They reflect that while methodologically he has remained in the mainstream of English analytic tradition, his views have changed considerably as he adopted the notion of universal salvation early on in his intellectual career and, more recently, as he has taken up the issues of religious pluralism.

For further autobiographical details, see Hick's *God Has Many Names* (London: The Macmillan Press, 1980), pp. 1-10; "Pluralism and the Reality of the Transcendent," *The Christian Century*, Vol. 98, No. 2 (Jan. 81), pp. 45-48; and *The Center of Christianity* (New York: Harper and Row, Publishers, 1978), p. 10.

[2]Many philosophers would disagree with what has just been said and perhaps go no further. They do not think that God is an ontological reality to which language can meaningfully refer. Although people talk about various conceptions of God, it is not thought that experience supports such talk. Hick on the other hand believes that talk about God may be true because it corresponds to an omnipotent benevolent God who can be known through finite modes of human experience. Examination of the conceptual mechanism by which Hick tries to substantiate his belief is the concern of this study.

[3]John Hick, *Death and Eternal Life* (New York: Harper and Row, Publishers, 1980), pp. 29-30. Though Hick only mentions here that he intends to use affirmations that may be at least partly true or false when comparing different religions, that he thinks the truth or falsity of such statements is in some degree a matter of the possibility of their empirical verification is found explicitly in *The Center of Christianity* (New York: Harper and Row, Publishers, 1978), pp. 97-98, and note 4 below. For an example of Hick using the possibility of eschatological verification as a criterion for meaningful comparisons of religious traditions, see *Death and Eternal Life*, p. 327.

With regard to his global theology, it should be emphasized that Hick is not trying to construct a single world religion. He thinks the different human cultures evidence a range of mentalities that require different religions. Though a single world religion is not possible, he yet thinks that a world or global theology may be approached. It would consist of hypotheses designed to interpret the experience of mankind within the great streams of religious life (see *God Has Many Names*, p. 8). Theology thus seems to stand in relation to religious language as a language about another language. Accordingly, when I refer to propositions as being either theological or religious, I will assume those that are theological are metalinguistically related to those that are religious. Theological propositions will thus be understood to be a part of a language about religious language, the truth or falsity of a theological proposition depending upon its depicting what the religious language actually purports. My concern will not be so much with theological statements as it will be with those religious assertions which in some way suppose God as their referential reality or object.

[4]My introductory remarks here about Hick's account of language will be developed further in chapters II and III. Hick's views on these matters can be found in *Faith and Knowledge* (2nd ed.; Cleveland: Fount Paperbacks, 1978), ch. 8; "Theology and Verification," in *The Logic of God*, ed. by Malcolm Diamond and Thomas Litzenburg, Jr. (Indianapolis: The Bobbs-Merrill Company, Inc., 1975), pp. 188-208; "Eschatological Verification Reconsidered," *Religious Studies*, Vol. 13, No. 2 (June 77), pp. 189-202; *God and the Universe of Faiths* (London: The Macmillan Press, Ltd., 1973), chs. 2 and 3.

[5]Hick, *Faith and Knowledge*, pp. 172-173.

[6]Hick, *God and the Universe of Faiths*, p. 27.

[7]Ibid., p. 11.

[8]Ibid., p. 25.

[9]See, for example, Norman Kemp Smith's translation of Kant's *Critique of Pure Reason* at B1 and A19-A20. With regard to Kant's distinction between phenomena and noumena, see B303, B305-306, A255 and B344.

[10]John Hick, "Towards a Philosophy of Religious Pluralism," *Neue Zeitschrift fur systematische Theologie*, Vol. 11, No. 2 (1980), p. 141.

[11]Ibid., p. 142.

[12]Ibid., p. 146.

[13]Ibid., p. 143.

[14]Ibid., pp. 142-147.

[15]Hick, *God and the Universe of Faiths*, pp. 43, 47.

[16]Ibid., pp. 37-52.

[17]Hick, *Faith and Knowledge*, p. 143.

[18]Hick, *God and the Universe of Faiths*, p. 47. Perhaps it is of interest here that, if one asks what is the relationship of the infinite, self-existent creator to the material environment, Hick seems to be willing to opt for an idealist answer. Hick implies that Berkeley's theory may be a likely

account of the metaphysical status of our present world (*Death and Eternal Life*, pp. 275-276).

[19]John Hick, *Evil and the God of Love* (San Francisco: Harper and Row, Publishers, 1978), p. 5, and Hick's "Eschatological Verification Reconsidered," p. 190.

[20]See, for example, Kai Nielson, *Contemporary Critiques of Religion* (London: The Macmillan Press, 1971); Terence Penelhum, *Problems of Religious Knowledge* (London: The Macmillan Press, 1971), Rem Edwards, *Reason and Religion: An Introduction to the Philosophy of Religion* (New York: Harcourt Brace Jovanovich, Inc., 1972), and so on. A fairly extensive list of such works is found in Hick's "Eschatological Verification Reconsidered," p. 191. The arguments in these works are often directed toward Hick's notion of eschatological verification, but some of them also deal with his doctrine of experiencing-as.

[21]Others have also tried to accommodate positivism. Michael Tooley has recently tried to challenge it on its own terms in his article, "Theological statements and the question of an empiricist criterion of cognitive significance," in *The Logic of God*, ed. by Diamond, pp. 481-524. Ian Ramsey has in the more modern empiricist tradition tried to show that some religious sentences are descriptive of facts. See his *Religious Language* (London: SCM Press Ltd., 1957), and *Christian Discourse* (London: Oxford University Press, 1965). I. M. Crombie is similarly known for his paper, "The Possibility of Theological Statements," in *Faith and Logic*, ed. by B. Mitchell (London: Allen and Unwin, 1957). Richard Swinburne's works, *The Coherence of Theism* (Oxford: Clarendon Press, 1977), *The Existence of God* (Oxford: Clarendon Press, 1979), and *Faith and Reason* (Oxford: Clarendon Press, 1981), complete a trilogy in which orthodox Christian beliefs are again defended within the British empiricist tradition.

[22]A. J. Ayer, *Language, Truth and Logic* (New York: Dover Publications, Inc., 1946), pp. 114-115.

[23]Hick mentions Feigl approvingly in "Eschatological Verification Reconsidered," p. 193.

[24]Herbert Feigl, "Confirmability and Confirmation," *Revue Internationale De Philosophie*, Vol. 5 (1951), pp. 268-279, and "Logical Positivism After Thirty-five Years," *Philosophy Today*, Vol. 8 (Winter 1964), pp. 228-245.

[25]Herbert Feigl, "The 'Orthodox' View of Theories: Remarks in Defense as well as Critique," in *Minnesota Studies in the Philosophy of Science*, Vol. IV: *Analysis of Theories and Methods of Physics and Psychology*, ed. by Michael Radner (Minneapolis: University of Minnesota Press, 1970), p. 6.

[26]Ibid., p. 7.

[27]Richard Swinburne, *An Introduction to Confirmation Theory* (London: Methuen, 1973).

[28]Hick, "Eschatological Verification Reconsidered," p. 194.

[29]Hick, "Theology and Verification," p. 191. The mechanism of

23

verification found here is later supposed and built upon in Hick's "Eschatological Verification Reconsidered" as he states on p. 191 of the latter. The notable modifications in the latter have to do with his Christology and religious pluralism. Hick now believes that the significance of one's religious awareness in the eschaton could be that of Hinduism, Buddhism, or any of the major religions.

[30]Hick, "Eschatological Verification Reconsidered," p. 195.

[31]Ibid., p. 199.

[32]Ibid., pp. 201, 202.

[33]Hick, *Philosophy of Religion* (2nd ed., Englewood Cliffs: Prentice-Hall, Inc., 1973), p. 93.

[34]The notion of eschatological verification was used by Ian Crombie, "Theology and Falsification," in *New Essays in Philosophical Theology*, ed. by Antony Flew and Alasdair MacIntyre (New York: The Macmillan Press, 1955), and it has been criticized by Paul Schmidt, *Religious Knowledge* (Glencoe, Illinois: The Free Press of Glencoe, Inc., 1961); William Blackstone, *The Problem of Religious Knowledge* (Englewood Cliffs: Prentice-Hall, Inc., 1963); and others (see Hick, "Eschatological Verification Reconsidered," p. 191).

[35]Hick, *Philosophy of Religion*, p. 1.

[36]Hick, *God Has Many Names*, p. 13. Hick further describes his theology as having "...a long and respectable ancestry, going back through Schleiermacher ultimately to the earliest fathers of the church, particularly Irenaeus..." (Ibid., p. 17).

[37]John Hick, *The Center of Christianity* (New York: Harper and Row, Publishers, 1978), p. 9. See also *God and the Universe of Faiths*, p. 92.

[38]Hick, *Death and Eternal Life* (New York: Harper and Row, Publishers, 1976), p. 53.

[39]Hick, *God and the Universe of Faiths*, p. 94.

[40]Ibid., p. 95.

[41]Ibid.

[42]Ibid.

[43]Ibid., p. 97.

[44]Hick, *The Center of Christianity*, pp. 9-13.

[45]Hick, "Eschatological Verification Reconsidered," p. 189.

[46]Hick, *God and the Universe of Faiths*, p. 97.

[47]Hick, *The Center of Christianity*, p. 64.

[48]Ibid., pp. 62-63.

[49]Ibid., p. 90. Hick's position on the problem of evil can best be seen in his well-respected work, *Evil and the God of Love*, pp. 243-386.

[50]Hick, *Philosophy of Religion*, p. 41.

[51]Ibid., p. 43.

[52]Hick, *The Center of Christianity*, p. 115.

[53]Hick, *Philosophy of Religion*, p. 43.

[54]Stephen T. Davis, ed., *Encountering Evil* (Atlanta: John Knox Press, 1981), p. 66. Hick derives his notion of a *bardo* phase from the Tibetan Book of the Dead. For detailed discussion of this notion, see *Death and*

Eternal Life, pp. 400-404.

[55]Hick, *Death and Eternal Life*, p. 252.

[56]Hick, *Philosophy of Religion*, p. 60.

CHAPTER II

PRELIMINARY ISSUES

One of the underlying issues of this chapter is whether or not assertions about God are to be viewed as capable of some degree of empirical verification, that is, whether talk about God should be understood to connect logically with concepts that are derived from experience of the divine transcendent entity to which they sometimes seem to refer.[1] Hick, as we have seen, believes that it is important that such a connection be shown to obtain. Not everyone agrees. In this chapter, we will consider two different approaches to this issue, each of which rejects the idea that religious assertions must be empirically verifiable.

One group, represented by Alvin Plantinga and George Mavrodes, opposes religious verificationism from a theistic point of view. They agree with Hick that some religious language is cognitive, or as Plantinga would have it, that belief in God is properly basic, but they reject Hick's contention that talk about God must be empirically verifiable. They seek to explain the cognitivity of religious language in other ways.[2] The second group, representing what might be called a Wittgensteinian point of view, is sometimes atheistic.[3] In this case religious language is believed to be false if taken literally, and accordingly, such Wittgensteinians often suggest that the significance of theistic language is of a noncognitive sort, though some thinkers in this camp would deny the distinction between cognitive and noncognitive uses of language.

Despite the clear differences between these two groups, they both deserve consideration in view of their common relation to Hick. For each group, in its own way, questions Hick's contention that religious language is meaningful only if it is empirically verifiable. But before considering some of their questions, I will first clarify the distinction between cognitive and noncognitive types of discourse.

1. Cognitive Versus Noncognitive Language

Hick believes there are two basic conceptions of the universe which he calls humanism and transcendent theism. We have seen in chapter I that there is an issue between these two conceptions that may present itself as a problem concerning religious language. "In a sentence," says Hick, "the issue is whether distinctively religious utterances are instances of the cognitive or of the non-cognitive uses of language."[4]

According to this distinction, religious language should be understood to be either cognitive or noncognitive, depending upon whether or not those who are using it are actually talking about a reality beyond their own thinking. It is cognitive if it refers to the existence of a divine ontological reality that actually exists outside the mind of the one speaking or writing, and it is noncognitive if it only expresses concepts that do not refer to anything outside one's mind. Cognitive language must convey information or indicate facts by making statements that are either true or false. And to be true or false, we have seen that talk about God (or anything) must logically lay itself open to experiential confirmation or disconfirmation. Otherwise, if there is no objective experiential distinctive with regard to which a statement might be verified, meaning or systematic use of it should be thought to lie within the range of its noncognitive usage. Its meaning might be typical of poetry, exclamations, greetings, and any other nonindicative, noncognitive use of language. Contemporary skeptics who use this terminology will acknowledge, says Hick, that the historical assertions of religious language, such as that there were men named Solomon and Jesus, are fact asserting, that is, are cognitive statements. That part of a proposition that makes reference to God, however, if it is incapable of being verified, would on this account be considered noncognitive.[5]

Hick fully realizes that there are many other uses of religious language that may be found on either side of this distinction. Hick says there is a network of possible distinctions which includes elocutionary forces of many variations. They may be commissive, verdictive, behabitive, and so forth, "...all of which can be detected within the range of religious utterances, and none of which is directly assessed in terms of truth value."[6] But he thinks the dichotomy induced by distinguishing cognitive from noncognitive religious statements is most basic, for it allows such statements as "God loves mankind" to be evaluated as either true or false. If there is no possibility that this type of statement about God can be true, he thinks the core conviction of most religions (that God exists) would be lost, because people would not continue to worship and serve a nonexistent entity (a mere expression or concept).[7]

Hick therefore wants to preserve the distinction between cognitive and noncognitive types of language. Given this distinction, he can attempt to save the factual quality of religious language via his notion of eschatological verification. He believes, as we have seen, that if humans survive death, post-mortem experience may eventually confirm for everyone the truth (or falsity) of religious language. Meanwhile, prior to this eschatological experience, Hick thinks religious discourse should carry factual or cognitive status because of its prediction of this eschatological situation that may in the future either be confirmed or disconfirmed. Hick's effort to save the core conviction of Christianity thus seems to depend upon a real distinction between cognitive and noncognitive types of language. If there were no distinction of this kind, his notion of eschatological verification would no longer serve its intended purpose.

But Neo-Wittgensteinian thinkers such as W. T. Jones have challenged this distinction.[8] Jones argues it involves the unnecessary assumption that of the two basic kinds of languages, the cognitive type that is typically employed by the sciences is superior. As a result, there is a great deal of tension between the sciences and the humanities, because those who are oriented toward the sciences tend to categorize the humanistic language of aesthetics, ethics, and religion as a second-class sort that does not need to be taken as seriously as the scientific type.

What has generated this tension, thinks Jones, is the supposed difference in kind between cognitive and noncognitive languages, whereas a better description would only recognize differences of degree. Jones argues that language should be understood in terms of a linguistic spectrum of usage that does not elevate one type of language over another. At one end of this spectrum are the languages of the sciences that mostly designate facts, while at the other end are the languages of the humanities that usually express what people feel. But facts may be designated and values may be expressed at either end of this spectrum. Jones says these designative and expressive components should be found to be blended throughout the spectrum of use. Rather than there being two separate "cognitive" and "noncognitive" labels, we should think of there being a linguistic continuum that ranges from having a high degree of designative (factual) components (yet still including expressive components) at one end, to a high degree of expressive (emotive) components (while still including designative components) at the other end.[9]

Affecting one's use of this spectrum is the nature of one's experience or perceptual field. Jones suggests that one's experience is composed of foreground (anything that we now directly experience) and background (anything we hope, suspect, believe, or know about what we now experience). The amount of complexity and richness of a background and its relationship to foreground, or even the transformation of one into the other, is thought to vary tremendously from person to person and from group to group. The composition of foreground and background structures and the line of demarcation between them is always in flux.[10] Though there are standard foregrounds which are a function of the predominant concepts of a society, Jones believes these naturally change over a period of time, depending upon the background structure a society happens to prefer.[11]

A person's experience, composed as it is of some combination of foreground and background, will determine which of the plurality of languages will be most useful to a person. In keeping with the nature of experience, there are what Jones calls basic value complexes implicit in each language that determine the function of a designative component of a language. The scientific languages, for example, have a background structure aimed at ascertaining facts and therefore contain value complexes that emphasize this background, while the background and the value complexes of the language of the humanities are more expressive.[12] Assuming Jones' analysis is correct, when someone insists upon using a background structure that requires a strict dichotomy between noncognitive language in contrast to highly designative cognitive scientific language, this person is, according to Jones, mistakenly applying the standards generated by the value complexes of one language to another in which they have no application. Evaluated by the value complexes of scientific language, noncognitive uses of language are written off as inferior because they are incapable of being "true" or "false."[13]

Jones to the contrary wants to avoid elevating any one type of language by understanding it in terms of its usefulness in meeting an individual's needs. Human needs are seen to vary according to complex drive patterns that most basically stem from the likes of hunger, thirst, sexual desire, and drowsiness, as well as a primary operative drive of curiosity.[14] Jones thinks we like to straighten out puzzles and clear up ambiguities, and that the type of language a person uses to do this will be affected both by this individual's perception of the nature of the object (involving foreground and background structures) and by the overall configuration of this person's drive complex when curiosity is aroused. One might, for instance, be more inclined to talk about cloud-like characteristics on the horizon using factually designative language if one is concerned about a prolonged drought than would another person who at the same place and time (knowing nothing about the need of rain) is completely taken up

31

with the beauty of the sunset.[15]

The type of language that best relates to one's drive pattern will accordingly be more or less appropriate, or truthful, depending upon one's needs and desires and awareness at the moment. By thus defining truth-seeking in terms of need-reduction or complex drives such as the desire to reduce curiosity, Jones hopes to get the notion of truth off any one pedestal while also affirming its importance in meeting human needs. We see then that the truth of a proposition is for Jones a matter of the varying conditions of the complex foreground/background structure of one's culture-bound experience.

Jones accordingly thinks the cognitive or fact-oriented use of language with which Hick is often concerned is subtly misleading. It reflects the primary truth-seeking drive or need to get clear about something, which aspect of its function is fundamental because it enables us to ascertain the facts and thus to satisfy our curiosity about the world. Yet the danger here, as is also the case to a lesser degree with all language, is that we may not be aware of the metaphysical beliefs and presuppositions (the make-up of the foreground and background structures) by which the truth of this language is formulated.[16] Any one version of what constitutes factual language cannot function, therefore, as the primary language for all contexts, for each context has its own version of factuality. People who are aware of the limitations of a particular context, says Jones, will not find fact-oriented language troublesome.[17]

The fact-oriented languages of the sciences obviously have the highest proportion of designative components, but Jones thinks that the expressive humanistic languages of ethics, aesthetics, and religion are just as important. The humanistic languages function to focus a person's feelings with precision, though obviously not the designative precision of science. Jones thinks it is a precision that clarifies some powerful but obscurely felt affect, with the result that a person may find a release of tension through finding an order to a welter of his or her impressions. Macbeth's "A little water clears us of this deed" may, for instance, express a guilt-ridden person's felt need for purification from some disruptive way

32

of living. The clarification and order this type of expressive assertion brings to one's impressions is one of the marks, says Jones, of cognition.[18]

But this is not what Hick means by cognitivity. When he is dealing with the distinction between cognitive and noncognitive types of language, Hick understands cognitivity with explicit reference to that use of language which corresponds to experience of an objective reality that has arisen from outside a person's mind. I should point out, however, that although cognitive language is primary in Hick's way of thinking, he nevertheless believes that noncognitive language is also valuable. He says it is a means for the believer to express awareness of the mysteries that surround the facts of religion. He perhaps places as much emphasis upon the importance of noncognitive language as Jones would place upon expressive language.[19]

The difference between Jones' designative and expressive components and Hick's cognitive and noncognitive components is that the latter are distinguished by a line of demarcation established by the facts of experience. Hick's thought entails that there is such a line as a result of the mind's confrontation with the separate independent reality of the world. There is no such sharp distinction between minds and reality in Jones' approach.[20] Jones believes rather, as we have seen, that while we must distinguish between what is real and illusory, this distinction will vary according to foreground/background structures that may always change. Conceivably, what one society believes to be real, another society may believe is illusory, in accord with their basic needs. I will assume, for the purpose of my argument, that Jones is correct.

Bringing Jones' view to bear upon the issues of religious discourse, Jones seems to be confident that his description of the function of language will alleviate some of the strain between secular and religious thinkers. Jones thinks "it is easy to see why a man who once believed (literally) in a transcendent Reality beyond experience and who then came to disbelieve in it, would feel despair."[21] Jones says "it results... from first taking religious language literally and then concluding that, since it can't be literally true, it must be literally false."[22]

To the contrary, Jones suggests that

> ...the experience of meaningfulness (the suffusion of experience with value and significance) does not depend on assertions about transcendent Reality being literally true. Indeed, the experience of meaningfulness depends less on beliefs of any kind than on commitment to something we think...worth exerting ourselves for.[23]

Jones thinks "...many men today have such low-level criteria for the satisfactoriness of explanations that they are content with vague reassurances to the effect that God is still in his heaven and all is therefore right with the world."[24] And Jones goes on to say that his book is not addressed to these people. Talk about a transcendent being beyond our experience is far from designative, and has become, thinks Jones, an expression of the speaker's experience of a powerful affect.[25]

But in saying this, is Jones being sensitive to the value complexes indigenous to the religious language which Hick feels a need to use? How can Jones be sure that a transcendent God cannot enter into an individual's experience and therefore become a designative component of this individual's religious language?[26] Some types of religious language naturally include a high degree of designative factual components and accordingly the possibility of being true or false. Christians, Buddhists, Hindus, Jews, Muslims, Sikhs, and many other types of religious people feel that their religion indicates something of the actual structure of reality. The scriptures and creeds of these religions are not thought to represent arbitrary projections of desires and values but rather discourse which designates the actual divine basis of human existence. Those who intend their religious language to designate such things might yet think that some religious language is more expressive in function, and they might approve of Jones' attempt to show that expressive components are as important as designative ones. But Hick for one would still point to the designative uses of religious language and ask how well this language might function in this fact-oriented capacity.

An instance of this is Hick's insistence that to try to explain religious discourse strictly in terms of this world is to be unfaithful to the implications of this discourse concerning "how things are" and "what there is." For, says Hick,

> religious beliefs not only have connections with this familiar world, and with all our life within it, but also with aspects of reality transcending this world and our present earthly life. An obvious example is the religious faith in God's purpose to raise us to life again after death. So far as christian language is concerned it would be utterly arbitrary and dogmatic to cut out all references to resurrection, the life to come, heaven and...immortality, the fulfillment of God's purpose for men and women beyond as well as within this world.[27]

The question of Hick's ability to show that such religious language is factually designative is yet to come. In considering such matters as whether or not Hick's position need include eschatological verification, we will find ourselves dealing with this question. We do see, however, that Hick is intent upon a factually designative aspect of religious discourse to the extent that he leaves himself open to the criticism of those who think religious utterances are noncognitive. Hick intends for some of his religious assertions to designate both the possibility of experience of the unseen presence and purpose of God as well as the possibility of continued conscious existence after death. These hypotheses are meant to be literally either true or false. The distinction between cognitive and noncognitive assertions thus serves to illustrate how certain religious assertions should be understood. Hick believes that this distinction illustrates what must be entailed by factual religious discourse, and further, that it is eschatological verification that establishes religious language as the factual cognitive type.

The question of the correctness of Jones' analysis of language remains, but this question is outside the scope of my work. Were Jones to have shown that religious assertions cannot properly contain a highly designative component, we would need to examine his view further, for then Hick's approach to questions of religious fact would have become irrelevant for reasons other than those I will advance later on in this study. But we have only found that the cognitive versus noncognitive terminology may be inappropriate if language is, as Jones would have it, a mix of both designative and expressive elements. Hick in this event can incorporate the terminology of Jones, so that what is referred to as the designative component within theistic discourse will still obviously be dominant to the point of warranting some sort of distinction between factual and nonfactual usage of this language. As the possibility of the factual character of religious utterances can be brought into Jones' view of language in terms of designative components, the relevance of eschatological verification therefore seems to remain.

I should note again that Hick wants to leave plenty of room for noncognitive religious utterances. He thinks that in scriptures and creeds there is a large admixture of both the cognitive and noncognitive elements. He believes first that it is

> ...vitally important to maintain the genuinely factual character of the central affirmations of the Christian faith; and [second],...given a basic structure of factual belief, there is ample scope for the nonfactual language of myth, symbol and poetry to express the believer's awareness of the illimitable mysteries which surround that core of religious fact.[28]

But given that religious language may or may not be cognitive in nature, and that many people do not experience either their lives or the world in relation to a transcendent God, Hick thinks the humanist has cause to issue a challenge.

Though some religious people are conscious of a transcendent divine presence and purpose, since the world is the same whether or not we suppose it to exist in God's presence, and since history is the same whether or not we describe it as fulfilling God's purposes, the humanist or the secularist may well believe that, when religious language is used cognitively to refer to God's existence, it is cognitively meaningless. The humanist might think that religious language is useful, as we have seen, as it may do something to assuage a psychological need of a speaker, but it would be thought to include no claim of substance concerning the objective nature of a divine element of the universe.[29]

36

2. Plantinga and Mavrodes

When the skepticism of the secularist is brought against traditional Christian thinking by means of the requirements of an empiricist verification criterion of the sort we saw developed by A. J. Ayer in chapter I, Alvin Plantinga and George Mavrodes attempt to meet this challenge by arguing that such a criterion is untenable and therefore need not be followed. One of the effects of thus rejecting the requirements that some verificationists try to place upon religious language is to eliminate that which necessitated the notion of eschatological verification. For if religious language that presupposes or entails the existence of God is factually meaningful apart from the requirements of the possibility of empirical verification, as Plantinga and Mavrodes suppose it is, then Hick's conceptual mechanism for meeting the empiricist challenge is not needed. We will begin with Plantinga's argument before turning to that of Mavrodes.

In *God and Other Minds*, Plantinga reviews some of the various formulations of the verification principle that Ayer, Antony Flew, and others have argued should rule out the possibility of religious statements being meaningful.[30] Plantinga concludes that no one has succeeded in stating a version of the verification criterion that is plausible. In each attempt, the criterion is found either to include statements that the verificationist finds undesirable or to exclude statements which are obviously meaningful.[31] Were the verificationist to find a criterion with which he or she was satisfied, Plantinga would be dissatisfied if it excluded religious assertions. For although it might be suitable for scientific and common sense statements, and it might specify properties that distinguish these from religious statements, according to Plantinga, the theist should not think that this distinction is sufficient to show that religious utterances are meaningless or logically out of order. More recently, Plantinga has taken the issue further by attempting to show why belief in God is legitimate apart from any verificationist scheme.[32]

Although I will not deal with Plantinga's argument for the rationality of religious belief, were it found to succeed, not only would Hick's attempt to meet the positivist challenge to religious belief via eschatological verification be unnecessary, his entire epistemological approach to questions of religious fact would be called into question. Though the present study will to some degree corroborate Plantinga's position, I should point out that I will proceed without much concern for whether or not a workable empirical confirmation criterion of cognitive significance might be developed, except as Hick ventures to argue what such a criterion must entail.

Pertinent to Hick's effort is the discussion of George Mavrodes as to why attempts to formulate a verification criterion of meaning have been unsuccessful. Mavrodes supposes that he is asked to determine that some statement p is meaningful by showing that there is a conceivable statement, experience, or state of affairs E that would verify it.[33] So he thinks that if he can determine that E is true, he must ask whether it is true that

(a)   E verifies that p.

But, argues Mavrodes, the truth of a statement of the form of (a) is in part a matter of what is filled in for p. Were E an experiment that would verify the special theory of relativity, and this theory p were replaced with some other p, perhaps the Mendelian theory of inheritance, E would not verify this replacement p. These two theories are so diverse that it is unlikely, thinks Mavrodes, that a single experiment would be relevant to the truth of both of them. But how can we know for which it is relevant? Mavrodes observes that unless he understands the assertions made by the sentences that express the theory that is filled in for p, he is not in a position to be able to determine whether or not a certain experiment will verify it. Unless Mavrodes knows the meaning of p, and more importantly that p is meaningful, no matter what happens to be the context of p (it might be a religious statement), he claims that he will not be able to know the truth of a statement having the form of (a). A statement of this form will be unintelligible to a person who does not understand p. If one is thus inclined to think that p is meaningless, this person should also think that a statement like (a) is meaningless. Mavrodes thus concludes that verification requires an impossible task. He does not think that we can

> ...discover that a given statement or sentence is verifiable in principle *before* we understand what assertion is being expressed in it. And therefore we cannot make verifiability a criterion for determining, in disputed cases, whether the given statement or sentence is cognitively meaningful.[34]

Some verificationists would perhaps do well to try to cope with Mavrodes' thinking, but it seems Hick has already taken the relevant issue into consideration.[35] When we explore what Hick thinks is involved in the verification of an assertion in the next chapter, we will find that his position does not exclude that a person can know the meaning of an assertion prior to its verification. To the extent that Hick believes one can distinguish between cognitive and noncognitive elements in religious language, one must understand the meaning of what is being expressed by an assertion before one can know how to classify it. Implied in Hick's thinking is thus that we can know the meaning of an assertion without having verified it. Only when one denies that a cognitive assertion at least corresponds to the possibility of indirect confirmation does Hick think that one is speaking meaninglessly. And Mavrodes might agree.

Mavrodes' contention applies to the early verificationist who argued that a nonanalytic factual statement is meaningful if and only if it can be verified empirically. Hick is not, however, holding this earlier position. His more recent formulation of verification is not so restrictive. Nonfactual or noncognitive assertions might be meaningful, though the meaning would be of a different sort than that understood by a factual assertion. As we will see, the character of meaning that Hick believes we apprehend of objects and situations is thought to be a product of both the mind and that which gives rise to conscious experience. In advancing this Kantian thesis, Hick seems to allow for meaningful assertions that are so because they relate only to one's consciousness and not to the world. Such an assertion would be the noncognitive type discussed earlier. But if religious assertions about God are intended to be cognitive, we have seen that he believes there must be a divine reality to which they refer. To see more exactly how assertions are thought to do this, we turn now to the question of Hick's understanding of that in which cognitivity consists.

NOTES

[1]There are of course contrary conceptions of God. The Whiteheadian god of process theology does not have the same infinite attributes as does Hick's God. Hick believes that God is limitlessly powerful, good and loving, and that this traditional conception of God is metaphysically more satisfying than the god of process theology (see, for example, Hick's critique of process theodicy in *Encountering Evil*, ed. by Stephen T. Davis [Atlanta: John Knox Press, 1981], pp. 122-123). My concern will be restricted to Hick's conception of God, the infinite nature of which Hick acknowledges cannot be given by experience. That God is infinite, says Hick, is a conclusion of natural theology (see "Eschatological Verification Reconsidered," *Religious Studies*, Vol. 13, No. 2 [June 77], p. 199). To my knowledge, Hick has not yet produced this bit of natural theology. But other contemporary philosophers have argued that a traditional conception of God is coherent. See Richard Swinburne, *The Coherence of Theism* (Oxford: Clarendon Press, 1977), and Stephen T. Davis, *Logic and The Nature of God* (London: The Macmillian Press, 1983). An introductory account of the issues is found in Ronald H. Nash, *The Concept of God* (Grand Rapids: Zondervan Publishing House, 1983). Hick has himself argued that the conception of God as a factually necessary being or a sheer, ultimate, unconditioned reality, without beginning or end (rather than a logically necessary being) is religiously satisfying and logically coherent. (See both Hick's *God and the Universe of Faiths* [London: The Macmillan Press, Ltd., 1973] ch. 6 and "God as Necessary Being," *Journal of Philosophy*, Vol. 57 [1960], 725-734).

[2]Alvin Plantinga has argued in *God and Other Minds* (London: Cornell University Press, 1967), that it is as rational to believe in God as it is to believe in other minds. He tries to show that arguments for other minds depend upon analogy in the same way as does the teleological argument for the existence of God. For a good critique of Plantinga's views, see Marie-Louise Frequegon, "God and Other Programs," *Religious Studies*, Vol. 15 (1979), pp. 83-89. More recently, in his *The Nature of Necessity* (Oxford: The Clarendon Press, 1974), among various issues, Plantinga has argued for the soundness of a modal version of the on-

tological argument and a solution to the problem of evil. But his means of dealing with those who deny the possibility of cognitive theistic claims are most recently and best seen in Alvin Plantinga and Nicholas Wolterstorff, eds., *Faith and Rationality: Reason and Belief in God* (Notre Dame: University of Notre Dame Press, 1983). For an account of Mavrodes' view, see chapter VI herein. Mavrodes has developed his thinking in both *Faith and Rationality* mentioned above and in *Belief in God: A Study in the Epistemology of Religion* (New York: Random House, 1970). For a similar discussion of the issues in religious epistemology, see Stephen T. Davis, *Faith, Skepticism, and Evidence: An Essay in Religious Epistemology* (London: Associated University Presses, Inc., 1978).

³Theists sometimes also utilize Wittgenstein's thinking, but not so as to affect this study. They assume that religious language is cognitive. See, for instance, Anthony C. Thiselton, *The Two Horizons: New Testament Hermeneutics and Philosophical Description* (Grand Rapids: W. B. Eerdmans Publishing Company, 1980), pp. 357-438. But many current views of religious language include the crude assumption, says Hick, that God does not exist. Such noncognitivist views accordingly restrict the use of religious language. They tend to agree that religious discourse may enrich human life as a special medium by which to express elusive feelings and concerns, but it must do this on a purely mundane level of human experience in which the notion of a real transcendent God can have no place. (See Hick, *God and the Universe of Faiths*, p. 18.) Representatives of this view differ over their understanding of the actual function of religious language. Hick points out that John Wisdom, J. H. Randall, and Peter Munz think religious discourse merely expresses a way of looking at the natural world; R. B. Braithwaite and T. R. Miles think it declares an intention to live in a certain way; W. Zuurdeeg thinks it belongs to a nonindicative class of convictional statements; and D. Z. Phillips thinks it is a special autonomous language that is indigenous to a religious way of living. (Ibid., p. 24. See also Hick's *Death and Eternal Life* [New York: Harper and Row, Publishers, 1980], p. 107.) Even though much of Hick's thinking stands in contrast to these various accounts of the function of religious language, it would not serve the purpose here to develop them, because they do not seem to have an impact on the internal coherence of his thinking, and moreover, that part of his work with which I am concerned may stand to show that these accounts are incorrect.

⁴Hick, *God and the Universe of Faiths*, p. 1.

⁵Ibid., pp. 1-17.

⁶Ibid., p. 2.

⁷Ibid., p. 21.

⁸W. T. Jones, *The Sciences and the Humanities: Conflict and Reconciliation* (Berkeley: University of California Press, 1965). I have chosen to use Jones' account, because, even though he makes the same crude

assumption as the philosophers listed in note 3 above, unlike them he specifically addresses the cognitive/noncognitive distinction upon which Hick depends, and Jones does this with a good deal of clarity. For an indication of the status of Jones' account and its relationship to the corpus of his work, see note 14 of chapter VI.

[9]Ibid., p. 153.

[10]Ibid., pp. 35-37. Jones says that what is now background may at another time be foreground; what is background for one person may at the same time be foreground for another; or part of a foreground may become background; or some people may have different backgrounds with respect to the same foreground, and so on (Ibid., p. 36). Also, the structuring of a foreground by means of a background is the product of some prior structuring of a foreground by a background, and the like (Ibid., p. 60). Jones often uses Galileo's discovery of the moons of Jupiter to illustrate some aspect of this process. On the night of January 7, 1610, Galileo saw three fixed stars in the night sky. "So would anyone else have seen fixed stars," says Jones,

> ...for the received opinion (a part of a standard background structure in 1610) was the belief (1) that there are but seven planets, and (2) that everything else in the night sky is a fixed star. Since the seven planets were already accounted for, these [three] new stars had, logically, to be fixed ones. Not that Galileo actually went through a process of reasoning. What he saw in his telescope were stars. But on the next night...when the fixed stars moved, there was no standard alternative background structure. (Ibid., p. 54.)

Perhaps by imagining what he would see from an immense distance, were he watching the moon turn about the earth, Galileo's experience was transformed. He now saw that what he once thought were fixed stars were actually moons of Jupiter. Galileo had made the shift to a new foreground, related functionally to a new background.

[11]Ibid., pp. 82-83. Jones believes also that standard foregrounds are relative to viewing procedures, which may include high-speed centrifuges, cloud chambers, particle accelerators, microscopes, or whatever (Ibid., p. 78).

[12]Jones says Macbeth's "A little water clears us of this deed" expresses values regarding forgiveness and purification. He thinks these values, or preference rules, as he sometimes calls them, link the term "water" both with a sacramental notion of purification and with the ordinary experience of a liquid substance, whereas the values or preference rules of science specify that water must unambiguously designate H_2O (Ibid., p. 204). The background structure of the sciences requires terms, thinks Jones, that reflect a strong interest in systematization and measure (Ibid., p. 192). The sciences value regularity of pattern, externality, neutrality, and separateness (Ibid., pp. 177-179). The values of scientific background structures are thus factual in nature and tend toward the designative pole of the linguistic spectrum, while the background structure and value complexes of the humanities tend toward the expressive pole.

[13]Ibid., pp. 155-157.

[14]Ibid., p. 110.

[15]Ibid., pp. 112-114. Jones points out here that one's drive pattern may be quite complex. There may be competing drives of various degrees of intensity and importance. For example, one may feel hungry while trying to diet, or one may want to avoid a certain kind of food to economize or to keep from illness.

[16]Ibid., p. 140.

[17]Ibid., pp. 101-104.

[18]Ibid., p. 208.

[19]Hick, *God and the Universe of Faiths*, p. 23.

[20]Jones believes we should abandon dualistic metaphysics because it has caused conflict between the scientific and the humanistic conceptions of life. He is not saying that a dualistic approach is mistaken, for he does not think that "true" or "false" are terms with which a theory can be appropriately characterized. He believes a dualistic metaphysics is dysfunctional and uneconomical, for if the world is what it is in complete distinction from our minds, different world views such as Hick's and A. J. Ayers', for example, must always contend with each other (*The Sciences and the Humanities*, pp. 28-29). Jones is recommending, instead, a description of experience that has both subjective and objective connotations, but which is not committed exclusively to either (Ibid., pp. 33-34). Hick, on the other hand, is committed to dualistic metaphysics. He argues for mind/body dualism, for instance, in *Death and Eternal Life*, pp. 112-126. We do not need to concern ourselves with a comparison of Hick and Jones on this issue, for if Jones' arguments were found to be superior, as we will see shortly, Hick could still assert his notion of eschatological verification by way of Jones' description of language.

[21]Jones, *The Sciences and the Humanities*, p. 270.

[22]Ibid.

[23]Ibid.

[24]Ibid., p. 143.

[25]Ibid., p. 271.

[26]Jones might say it is incoherent to speak of an experience of something that transcends experience. But Hick could reply that an infinite, transcendent, omnipotent being can somehow accommodate the finiteness of the human mode of experience. Hick's means of doing this include his doctrine of experiencing-as and his arguments from natural theology, as mentioned in note 1 above. If Hick cannot formulate such a reply, his belief in the literal reality of an infinite transcendent God would be jeopardized.

[27]Hick, *God and the Universe of Faiths*, p. 34. See also *Death and Eternal Life*, p. 156.

[28]Hick, *God and the Universe of Faiths*, pp. 22-23.

[29]Hick, "Eschatological Verification Reconsidered," p. 189.

[30]Plantinga, *God and Other Minds*, pp. 156-158.

[31]Ibid., p. 163.

[32]Alvin Plantinga and Nicholas Wolterstorff, eds., *Faith and Rationality: Reason and Belief in God* (Notre Dame: University of Notre Dame Press, 1983).

[33]Mavrodes, "God and Verification," pp. 223-229.

[34]Ibid., p. 229.

[35]Hick, "Eschatological Verification Reconsidered," p. 193. Hick says here that Plantinga's and Mavrodes' refusal to face the verificationist challenge is an example of unhelpful philosophical pedantry.

CHAPTER III

CONDITIONS OF FACTUAL MEANING

Hick believes a statement is cognitive in nature if it meets certain criteria of empirical verifiability. In this chapter, I will set forth the general characteristics of such criteria as well as some of their implications. We will find that cognitive use of language is based upon the empiricist concern that, for something to exist or to be the case, it must make a difference which can be experienced. We have already touched upon a few of the details of this empirical trait of nonanalytic cognitive assertions in the previous chapters, but we must now develop these details further. In so doing, we will prepare ourselves for the argument, in later chapters, that eschatological verification is unnecessary in Hick's system of thought, if not impossible.

My aim in this chapter will be primarily to explicate Hick's thinking. Except for the charge of relativism that I will introduce, most of my criticism will come in later chapters. We will begin with Hick's account of the basic conditions for factual meaning, after which we will look at several characteristics of the verifying experience upon which factual meaning depends. In light of these characteristics, we will then briefly consider the possibility and means of verifying statements about infinite divine attributes. Since Hick thinks that God has infinite attributes, this possibility must be realized if Hick is to maintain his current description of God, but the question as to whether Hick can successfully hold onto this description, I will suggest, is beyond the scope of this study. Most importantly in this chapter, we will look at the details of Hick's notion of eschatological verification in order to see why it supposedly satisfies the conditions of factual meaningfulness that some philosophers require of religious language. My concern for eschatological verification in this regard will be central to most of this chapter, though not always explicitly so.

1. Factual Meaning

Hick believes that the logical positivists never succeeded in developing a satisfactory verifiability criterion of factual meaningfulness, but he does not think that the insight that motivated their quest was illusory. "On the contrary," says Hick, "the central core of the positivist contention seems undeniable."[1] Formulating this contention, he states that to assert a factual statement p

> ...is to assert an in-principle-observable difference between the actual universe and a possible universe which differs from it only in that in the latter it is true that not-p. That there is such a difference constitutes p a factual statement; and to observe the features of the universe which differentiate it from a possible universe in which not-p, is to verify p. Accordingly to say that x exists or that p is the case, but to deny that the existence of x or the truth of p makes any such in-principle-experienceable difference would be to speak in a way that is pointless or meaningless.[2]

There are at least four factors of this account of factual meaningfulness that can be isolated. Hick is insisting that

(1)   to assert p is to assert that there is a difference which can be experienced, in principle at least, between the actual universe and a possible universe in which p is false.

Hick is specifying that the kind of statement that can be verified will in some way have to do with an actual state of affairs of the universe. A genuine empirical assertion must "...commit itself," says Hick, "to something being there which might conceivably turn out not to be there, or to some-

46

thing happening which might not happen."[3] Given this difference that can be experienced, he thinks that

(2) p is a factual statement precisely because there is a difference such as that in (1).

There are thus a raft of assertions that qualify as factual statements, because the experiential distinction in question need only be specified in principle. Though some propositions are false and as a result cannot be verified, Hick thinks nevertheless that such a proposition can be counted as factual if it is possible to specify circumstances which, were they to occur, would verify this statement. A statement about a mermaid is factual, for instance, in that it can be verified by sighting a sea creature with the upper body of a woman and the tail of a fish. Other propositions cannot be verified because at present it is physically impossible to do so. In such cases, Hick thinks the notion of prediction becomes central. For example, he believes that "...statements about the features of the dark side of the moon are rendered meaningful by the conditional predictions which they entail to the effect that if an observer comes to be in such a position in space, he will make such-and-such observations."[4] That is, although one is not able to base the status of a proposition upon actual observation, something can be experienced in principle if we can specify what would count as an observation or experience of it. If we can do this, a proposition may be factual though as yet unverified. For, as Hick believes,

(3) to observe the difference asserted by p between the actual universe and a possible universe is to verify p.

An assertion may accordingly be factual, even though it has never been verified. There is thus a distinction between factual statements and statements that have been verified. When an assertion is verified, it is then known by someone to be factual. It no longer only has the character of a factual proposition; it is now as a result of verification known to be a true assertion. But if a statement purports to have the factual qualities of (2) and yet cannot be verified according to (3), Hick says that it is nonsense, because

(4) p is meaningless if it purports to be cognitive but cannot in principle be verified.

A statement that is meant to be factual must be capable of empirical verification. A noncognitive statement, we have seen, is not thought to assert what can be observed, and (4) would thus not apply to it. This fourth factor does not seem to entail that noncognitive statements are meaningless (they may have a meaning of their own type), but only that statements which are supposed to be cognitive are not truly cognitive unless they assert an experiential difference with regard to an actual state of affairs of the world.

Hick is of course concerned with religious assertions that are thought to meet the criteria of (1) and (2). But Hick's problem is that many philosophers deny that the religious statements with which he is concerned can ever meet criterion (3). They argue in effect that there is no experiential state of affairs by which talk about a transcendent deity might be verified. They believe that an object that supposedly transcends the universe is beyond the realm of evidence, and that there is thus no possibility of empirical verification of propositions that refer to such an object.[5] According to (4), then, they think talk about a transcendent deity is meaningless if it purports to be cognitive. But to take exception to this claim, Hick attempts to come up with a state of affairs by which his religious assertions can be verified, in this way then maintaining the cognitive status of these assertions in keeping with (1) and (2).

To do this, as we have seen, Hick calls upon certain conditions predicted by post-mortem experience. He thus thinks he can legitimately postpone the verifying experience required of (3) while using religious language cognitively according to (1) and (2) during the interim. But it is not as though Hick thinks there can be no experiential confirmation in this life.

Hick believes that some people do currently experience the presence and purpose of a loving God, which experience may be sufficient to verify talk about God for these people. But this difference that can be experienced does not constitute evidence that will satisfy the skeptical philosopher. Hick thinks that since religious experience depends upon and is related supplementally to naturalistic experience of the universe, people can legitimately experience the universe either in light of their religious experience or else purely naturalistically.[6]

As I will substantiate in the next chapter, in Hick's way of thinking, the universe is much like one of the ambiguous puzzle pictures that Wittgenstein used as an illustration of things that can appear to an observer in more than one way. Jastrow's duck-rabbit drawing, for example, looks like a duck from one direction, or, when it is rotated about ninety degrees, like a rabbit. Similarly, the universe may be experienced either theistically or naturalistically in Hick's view. The experienced difference, in either case, is an appropriate experience of the data of the universe itself. The experiential difference by which the theistic account of the universe is verified thus to some degree confirms the theist's religious beliefs, while the skeptical philosopher who has no such experience is most satisfied with the naturalistic interpretation of the universe.

Weighing against the theist's interpretation of the universe, however, is the problem of evil and suffering in the world. As pointed out in the first chapter here, Hick believes it is right for the naturalist to think that if there is a good God who is not limited in ability to affect the affairs of the universe, then there should be no pain and suffering in the world. The naturalist believes that God should be opposed to evil in such a way that evil would not exist if there were in fact a good, omnipotent God. Since evil does exist, the naturalist concludes that either God does not exist or perhaps God is not omnipotent.[7] Even those who supposedly do experience God will, as a result of the pain and suffering in the world, thinks Hick, be prone to disbelieve that God is benevolent.[8]

It is chiefly these reasons, namely, (1) that the world is religiously ambiguous and (2) that evil circumstances may cause people to doubt the truth of the theistic interpretation of the universe, that Hick believes necessitate the concept of eschatological verification as a means of substantiating the factual quality of assertions about God. Hick's views in this regard will become more apparent when we examine eschatological verification more carefully at the end of this chapter. But first we should develop Hick's understanding of the nature of the verifying experience, for as we look at the characteristics of the verifying experience, what must be the function of eschatological verification will be clarified.

2. Characteristics of the Verifying Experience

The state of affairs a person may imagine or specify as a verifying experience for some proposition will depend in part upon the subject matter and the capacity of the one imagining. There are several aspects of Hick's thinking by which he characterizes and describes the nature of a rational observer's interaction with the subject matter. I will divide my discussion of these general characteristics into five segments.

First, Hick believes that we each live in our own phenomenal world which is nevertheless based upon objective reality. We are not sure "how we are conscious of sensory phenomena as constituting an objective physical environment; we just find ourselves interpreting the data of our experience in this way."[9] Our experience of the world's circumstances is always "...in terms of the concepts by which we apprehend (or of course misapprehend) objects and situations as having this or that character of meaning."[10] Hick thinks "...the world as we perceive it is real, not illusory; [sic] but it is the appearance to us of that which exists in itself outside our experience of it."[11] The world of colors, temperatures, sounds, and scents is truly out there, but as it is organized as phenomena of human perception, it exists independently as each individual's phenomenal awareness.

Second, Hick thinks that though we are real beings in a real environment, we only experience part of it, because we have cognitive equipment by which we experience our environment selectively. Our cognitive machinery consists of our sense organs and neuro-system along with the selecting and organizing activity of the mind/brain, this machinery, according to Hick, having a twofold function: it both shuts out and lets in awareness of our environment. Since we as psychophysical organisms have evolved under the pressure of continual struggle to survive, this evolutionary process has naturally caused us to have an outlook that is instinctively empirical and practical. It would be a fatal complication if we were so bemused by our environment that we could not react selectively to stimuli indicating food or danger.[12] Hick therefore thinks that our sensory equipment is selectively sensitive to only a minute portion of the total range of information that flows from our physical environment at any one time. Rather than seeing a swirling cloud of electrons as we look at a glass of water, we see a clear liquid that we drink. Both the senses and the mind/brain select and then relate and organize what we perceive into a version of the world that is enormously simplified. The result of this organizing that occurs within a framework of well-tried categories is a world that Hick thinks is simple enough to be successfully inhabited.[13]

Our sensory equipment, passed from parents to children genetically, determines our basic discriminatory ability to inhabit the world. Hick quotes C. D. Darlington, a contemporary geneticist, as he lists the human capacities, perceptual and otherwise, to which there is an important genetic contribution.

> Our hormone systems and hence our temperaments, whether sanguine, melancholy or choleric; timid or courageous; observant, reflective, or impulsive. Hence our social habits, whether solitary or gregarious; affectionate or morose; settled or nomadic; useful, deranged, or criminal; hence also the company we keep, and our capacities and directions of love and hatred. Our perception and appreciation of taste, touch and smell, sound and colour, harmony and pattern. Our capacities and qualities for memory, whether for sound, sight, number or form. Our kinds and degrees of imagination, visualization and reason. Hence our understanding of truth and beauty. Hence also our educability in all these respects, or lack of it and our capacity and choice in work and leisure.[14]

What Darlington has said here implies the possibility of differences about people, but that people usually successfully inhabit the world and report shared experience of the world seems to indicate to Hick that sensory and mental equipment is fairly uniform among most people with regard to basic levels of discrimination.[15] Hick notes that "...the material world compels us to cognize it substantially as it is or to suffer pain and even extinction."[16] Yet on social levels, Hick believes we behave according to values which are strongly influenced by a self-centered desire to preserve our own egocentric interests.[17] The differences in discrimination on the social level are thus accentuated.

Third, all conscious perceiving is thought to go beyond what the senses report to a significance that is not itself given to the senses.[18] By "significance," Hick says he means "...that fundamental and all-pervasive characteristic of our conscious experience which *de facto* constitutes it for us the experience of a "world" and not of a mere empty void or churning chaos."[19] Hick says he hopes there is no suggestion of anything occult in that feature of our experience which he is calling "significance."[20] He is only referring to the familiar intelligible character of experience that enables us to cope with our environment. Hick means to be opting for a general form of the Kantian thesis

> ...that we can be aware only of that which enters into a certain framework of basic relations which is correlated with the structure of our consciousness. These basic relations represent the minimal conditions of significance for the human mind. The totally non-significant is thus debarred from entering into our experience. A complete undifferentiated field, or a sheer "buzzing, booming confusion," would be incapable of sustaining consciousness.[21]

Except perhaps for early infancy or states of radical mental breakdown, the general characteristic of our experience to which "significance" refers is our awareness of the environment as having a quality of fundamental familiarity or intelligibility. "Significance, then," says Hick, "is simply the most general characteristic of our experience."[22]

Significance as so understood is a complex notion as it has to do with both objects and situations involving various times and places and processes of change. Although our interests may focus on a particular component within a situation, Hick thinks our normal mode of consciousness is of groups of objects standing in recognizable patterns of relations to each other, and it is the resulting situation taken as a whole that carries significance for us.[23]

Our assurance that any one interpretation of significance is accurate comes from our ability to act in accord with it. For acting on perceived significance verifies whether our environment is capable of being inhabited as though this significance were a real mode of experience. Hick believes that by acting on perceived significance or our interpretation of reality, "...we build up an apprehension of the world around us; and in this process interpretations, once confirmed, suggest and support further interpretations."[24] Some of the boundaries we find placed upon our actions are of course prescribed by a particular culture. Hick says "...that the main cultures of the world have been sufficiently different to constitute different ways of being human—including the Chinese, the Indian, the African, the Semitic and the Graeco-Semitic ways."[25]

Perceived significance will vary to some degree from person to person and especially from culture to culture, depending upon which aspect of perceived significance one might focus. But for the purpose here, we should primarily limit our concern to comparison of the perception of religious significance versus the secular type. Hick believes there are two different contrasting ways of experiencing the events of our lives,

> ...on the one hand as purely natural events and on the other hand as mediating the presence and activity of God. For there is a sense in which the religious man and the atheist both live in the same world and another sense in which they live consciously in different worlds. They inhabit the same physical environment and are confronted by the same changes occurring within it. But in its actual concrete character in their respective 'streams of consciousness' it has for each a different nature and quality, a different meaning and significance; for one does and the other does not experience life as a continual interaction with the transcendent God.[26]

Those who do experience life religiously are living by faith. This is faith in its primary sense, according to Hick, as a state which may be compared with standard instances of believing and knowing on the basis of perception. It is through faith, as a form of perceptual acquaintance, that an individual can recognize a religious significance by way of the mundane objects and events of life. I will return to Hick's concept of faith in the next chapter.

The implications of the three characteristics of the verifying experience that we have seen thus far (each individual has his or her own phenomenal awareness, this awareness is highly selective, and its significance is due to interpretation), suggest that knowledge is relative to each individual. Unless the cognitive machinery of humanity functions uniformly among most people, those who happen to be nonresponsive to certain segments of experience would have cause to be skeptical. Their insensitivity would preclude the possibility of direct verification of anything connected with a certain range of experience. Rightly they might think that talk about such matters is meaningless.

And Hick's position does entail the likelihood that the perceptual sensitivity and mind/brain capacity among humans is not the same, as was indicated by his use of Darlington earlier. Any individual's cognitive machinery is thought to be the result of millions of years of evolutionary development determined by humanity's needs for survival. Though there is some continuity between generations, there must also be change, the degree of which is not known. Hick says there is an

> ...enormous multiplication in the possibilities out of which a particular genetic code is selected when it is actualized by the union of a particular sperm with a particular egg. And it is out of this astronomical number of different potential individuals, exhibiting the kinds of differences that can occur between children of the same parents, that a single individual comes into being...[27]

complete with his or her unique cognitive machinery.

Drawing the discussion now toward the religious question, it seems to me that given the possible differences among individuals, Hick cannot insure that people have the same capacity to experience the world religiously or otherwise, so that, contrary to Hick's belief, the world may not be religiously ambiguous. An obvious indication that the world may not be religiously ambiguous is the fact that many people claim their experience of it provides grounds for theism. Hick would not deny that many well-respected thinkers have been so impressed by the structure and beauty of the world that they suggest a divine cause. The intricate complexity and interdependence of the systems of nature have often led people to speculate about an ultimate ground of the order and regularity of the universe, such as is found in the teleological argument. Richard Swinburne and other contemporary figures who support this approach may conceivably be compelled to do so, in Hick's way of thinking,[28] because their cognitive machinery is of a different sensitivity than that of the naturalist who does not experience the purported evidentualist grounds for theistic belief.

In Hick's view, then, that the naturalist lacks the experience and thus the concepts that correspond to the theist's discourse does not seem to establish that theistic experience is unrelated experimentally to the universe. The relationship between the theist and the naturalist might be like that between Newton's and Einstein's understanding of the significance of the universe. Though Einstein's view is now understood to be the richer conception, those scientists who resisted this move in many instances thought there were no experimental means by which to describe the issues and that Einstein's position was mostly a detrimental, mistaken bit of conceptual baggage.[29] Just as physicists eventually made the shift to a new paradigm, similarly, theists and people who become theists often claim to find their perceived significance of the universe verified by a new-found ability to interact successfully with their environment. And if the theist and the agnostic both find that their perceptions of the significance of the material environment are supported by the way in which they inhabit the material environment, it seems that the practicality of being able to act or live in accord with either of these perceptions of significance does not favor one over the other. Much as a measuring cup might be perceived to be merely a cup, what the theist perceives as God's creation might also be perceived to be a purposeless material environment. But the unifying factor provided by the perceived object itself would not in any way exclude the richer of these two perceptions. On this account, the theist does not experience the world much differently than does the naturalist, and the differences there are may be due to the extent to which the world is actually perceived.

I am not suggesting that the truth of theism is in fact

evidenced by the world. It may or may not be. What I am suggesting is that, whichever is the case, is, according to Hick's assumptions about the acquisition of information about the world, relative to the individual observer and that Hick is himself therefore in no position to say assuredly that the universe is religiously ambiguous. He should only say that some people experience the world theistically while others do not. Either of these interpretations of the data may occur more nearly on the social level than on the level of the material environment, thus reflecting an individual's personal bias, but it does not seem to me that Hick can substantiate that the world is equally supportive of either interpretation. Hick may concur, for what he actually argues is that both the naturalist and theistic interpretations are so comprehensive in scope (they are total interpretations), that they no longer stand in relation to any data by which they would be rendered more or less probable. Both encompass all of what is given. I will clarify and question Hick's notion of a total interpretation in the next chapter, and thus I will postpone much further consideration of the supposed ambiguous character of the universe until then. Turning now rather to a fourth and a fifth general characteristic of the verifying experience, we will see the extent of the relativism in Hick's system of thought.

Fourth, the imagined experience that may in principle verify a proposition may range in scale from providing complete and conclusive verification, says Hick, down through providing various degrees of confirmability.[30] Conclusive verification occurs when any grounds for doubt have been completely removed from a rational observer's mind. When there is no longer room for rational doubt about some proposition, one has acquired what Hick refers to as the point of cognitive conclusiveness. The nature of the situation that excludes rational doubt about the truth of some proposition will depend upon the context of the proposition in question. Propositions about a good and loving creator naturally occur in the context of the present supposedly religiously ambiguous world in which, as we have seen, there is a mixture of good and evil circumstances. "All that is good, beautiful, creative

56

and uplifting in the world-process agrees with and thus far confirms the belief in a good and loving creator, whilst pain and suffering, wickedness and ugliness are dissonant circumstances which thus far disconfirm that belief."[31] Hick thus believes it is often the circumstances of sin and suffering, ugliness and deprivation that presently leave room for doubt concerning the reality of God's presence and purpose.

Fifth, Hick thinks that verification may be simple or complex. It is simple if the difference made by the truth of an assertion is sufficiently specifically defined and localized in space and time. "For example, the difference made by there being a table in the next room can be registered by a single visual observation (perhaps supported by touching) so that 'There is a table in the next room' is close to exhibiting maximally simple verifiability."[32] Conclusive verification will occur in cases such as this through a single act of perception. On the other hand, verification is complex if the difference made by the truth of an assertion is variable in nature and/or diffused in extent. In this case its confirmation may require many cumulative observations.[33] For example, says Hick, that a man is honest "...cannot be verified by a single observation, for the experienceable difference made by his being an honest man is spread out over time and is also variable in the forms that it can take. The same is true of the theory of evolution, or indeed any large-scale scientific hypothesis."[34] Complex verification thus includes various indirect means of inference.[35]

But one of the problems we have seen is that whether some body of evidence is experienced as either confirming or disconfirming any given proposition may be relative to each individual. Hick has no way of insuring that one person has the same grounds as another for belief in or doubt of the truth of complex propositions, especially as such propositions occur on the social level. Personal judgment must enter into the evaluation of the data perceived to be either confirming or disconfirming of such propositions. And since the amount and quality of data required in either case may vary among individuals, it is not apparent then that Hick is able to specify what it is exactly that constitutes grounds for rational doubt for any one person regarding a complicated set of circumstances.

It seems that Hick's theory of confirmation thus allows a great deal to be said. So long as an individual can specify what in principle would count as verification of an assertion, it seems from what we have seen so far that this assertion should then be considered meaningful for this individual despite whether or not other people are able to sense the experiential difference by which its confirmation is supposedly brought about. For example, assuming Hick's account of verification describes what has actually gone on in the history of science, it was appropriate for Einstein to reject the experimental findings that Kaufmann and Miller used to refute the general theory of relativity.[36] It may be that Einstein was more sensitive and able with the data. Again, astronomers may disagree about which model of the universe best accounts for the available data because they are each more or less able to deal with the question.

Hick might contend, however, that I am assuming the disparity between the cognitive machinery of various individuals is greater than it actually is. I would reply that while I do not know how great the differences happen to be, there could conceivably be major differences, and it seems that there is currently no possibility of determining otherwise. Research in this area is dependent upon classification of scales of measurement that are limited by what is known about human physiology and various assumptions having to do with the properties of light, memory, electro-chemical exchange, the relationship between stimulus and consciousness, and so on. Precision and reliability of measurement is not always accurate, and most importantly, it may not even be possible. Measurement would be beyond experimental possibility if the data occur on the level of human consciousness. If, for example, individuals with the most developed cognitive machinery are consciously aware of more of reality than other people, perhaps because they are able to process all of the modes of sensual input simultaneously, the evidence of this ability would occur at the conscious level. Even if physical measurements could be obtained for the degree of an individual's sensitivity, examination of a person's consciousness of the data after it has been processed is not possible except as the individual reports it. The results would thus only be as accurate as the person's claim.

According to Hick's criteria of factual meaning, then, this person's claim would be meaningful for this individual because of his or her awareness of the experiential difference to which this claim refers, but this claim might mean a lot less to those who are incapable of an awareness of the experiential difference in question, unless they are willing to accept this person's claim. Hick's conditions of factual meaning may thus sometimes have little practical value for distinguishing factual statements or cognitive claims from noncognitive ones, and if anything, his distinction between simple and complex verification seems to open wide the class of statements that may pass as cognitive claims, as can be seen in Hick's purpose for advancing this distinction.

Hick believes his distinction between simple and complex verifiability is important as a means of avoiding a wrong approach to the verification of theistic statements. In contrast to a statement that can be verified through a single observation, such as one about objects in the next room, a statement about God cannot be verified in this same simple way. The infinite transcendent God is not thought to be localized in space and time. As we have seen, what we should look for, in Hick's view, is a development of our experience that will progressively confirm theistic statements to the point of there being no possibility of rational doubt of their truth.

Explaining this development that would supposedly enable one to progress toward cognitive conclusiveness is obviously no simple matter. Those who talk about their experience of God often do so via finite analogies. Corresponding to the notions of limited power, local presence, finite goodness, and human love, there is said to be a God with infinite attributes of omnipotence, omnipresence, perfect goodness, and infinite love. And since these infinite qualities are not given in finite human experience, philosophers such as Hume have often wondered how a finite individual could ever actually experience the infinity of God.

3. An Infinite God From a Finite Effect

In agreement with Hume, Hick does not think that one can affirm the infinity of God on the basis of perception alone. Hick says that "...God's alleged impingement upon his creation...is necessarily a finite impingement: power exerted non-destructively upon a finite object must itself be finite."[37] So Hick does not entertain theistic statements that treat infinite divine existence as though it were an isolable and bounded fact that is capable of verification by a single simple observation. Hick says,

> What we are seeking to verify is the truth of the theistic interpretation of the process of the universe; and this *verificandum* is embodied in more complex propositions such as "The theistic account of the character of the universe, and of what is taking place in its history," is true.[38]

Hick does not think that this type of proposition will bypass the question of the existence of God, nor is it designed to do so, "...for God must be referred to in giving an account of the meaning of 'theistic' in this context."[39] God "...will appear in this account as the supreme being who controls the process of the universe and who is bringing it to the end which he himself intends. But the infinite nature of his attributes—the infinity of his power, knowledge, love, etc.—are [*sic*] not involved in this account."[40]

Hick yet believes it is possible to establish the infinite attributes of God through arguments of natural theology such as those used by Thomas Aquinas. Whether or not these arguments will in fact support Hick's concept of deity is tangential to my thesis. If they do not, he might then change his concept of God. The more limited Whiteheadian god of process theology might be an option, for example.[41] But consideration of such possibilities is beyond the scope of this study. I am arguing that his effort to show the verifiability of religious statements about God is problematic. But before I develop my thinking, we should first see more explicitly what is entailed by Hick's notion of eschatological verification. It is this notion, Hick contends, that satisfies the philosopher's requirements for factual discourse about the nature and purpose of God.

4. Eschatological Verification

Hick uses a parable of two travelers to illustrate his concept of eschatological verification. A Christian and a nonbeliever are traveling together through the journey of life, both men being subject to the same material environment. The Christian does not experience anything that cannot be explained in natural terms. The difference between the two is that the Christian believes that the events of this journey are designed to make of him a worthy citizen when at last he completes his pilgrimage to a Celestial City, while the nonbeliever accepts none of this.[42] This parable, says Hick,

> ...is designed to make only one point: that Judaic-Christian theism postulates an ultimate unambiguous existence *in patria*, as well as our present ambiguous existence *in via*. There is a state of having arrived as well as a state of journeying, an eternal heavenly life as well as an earthly pilgrimage. The universe as envisaged by the theist, then, differs as a totality from the universe as envisaged by the atheist. However, from our present standpoint within the universe, this difference does not involve a difference in the objective content of each or even of any of its passing moments.[43]

In saying that the difference between the theist and the atheist involves the envisioning of the totality of the universe, Hick seems to be touching upon his notion of a total interpretation, which, as I have mentioned, we will consider in the next chapter. But we have already seen that his further claim that the difference between them involves no objective content of the universe is itself a claim that, based on what we have seen of Hick's thinking, has not been substantiated. This is due to the relativism at the center of his account of human experience. The person who supposedly perceives a cosmological, theological, or moral ground for theism, for instance, may presumably be doing so, even though the naturalist experiences no such ground.

The existence of God might accordingly be a bit like the existence of a quark or a neutron, complete with the attendant problems involved in establishing a connection between observation and theory. If so, Hick's parable is misleading in that it fails to model the requirements of religious language upon the same language usage as is found in the sciences. It may be that there are almost as many objective data by which to distinguish the viewpoint of the theist from that of the atheist as there are data distinguishing the scientists' view from the view of the skeptic of science. In the next chapter we will see more of this possibility.

Though Hick continues to use his parable of the travelers to illustrate his notion of eschatological verification, I should point out that in recent years his understanding of the circumstances that will constitute the eschatological end state has undergone somewhat of a change. According to Hick's original formulation of eschatological verification, after a person dies, he or she would awaken to some sort of new existence in which familiar characteristics of body and memory would indicate continued personal identity with the previous life. This person would meet relatives and friends and historical personages who are also known to have died, so that there could be no doubt that this is a post-mortem resurrection experience. Christian theism would by this experience be found to be the fulfillment of God's purpose for mankind as has been disclosed in Christian revelation. One feature of this original conception of the eschatological situation that would have made its fulfillment easy to recognize was the authoritative teaching of Christ. Hick believed that "an experience of the reign of the Son in the Kingdom of the Father would confirm that authority, and therewith, indirectly, the validity of Jesus' teaching concerning the character of God in his infinite transcendent nature."[44] But this original eschatological expectation has been revised.

Hick has become aware, he says, "...that it is far from clear that Jesus did in fact teach that God is infinite."[45] And it is also no longer apparent to Hick that Jesus is the only revelation of God. Having a new interest in religious pluralism, Hick wants to play down the dominance of Christ in traditional

Christianity in order to make room for the doctrinal systems and the authority figures of the other religions. Many of the other major world religions besides Christianity are now entertained as perhaps also providing legitimate paths to God. Hick says with regard to the plurality of religious options that in the

> future it may turn out that the root visions [the soteriological functions of major religions] were maps of different possible universes, only one at most of which is actualized; or it may turn out that they were analogous to maps of the same world drawn in radically different projections, each method of projection distorting reality in a different fashion and yet enabling the traveller successfully to find his or her way. But it is clear that the character of the universe and our place within it will become known to us, if at all, by experience and observation.[46]

Hick seems to be saying here that in the eschaton, we may find that only one of the various different religious prescriptions for salvation (soul-making) was correct, or we may find that they are all correct with the result that whatever religious path a person has chosen will have led this individual to God. With the exception of the new general de-emphasis upon Christ and the new general emphasis upon the plurality of religions, it is difficult to compare Hick's present understanding of the eschatological situation with his old one. He no doubt continues to believe that we will each recognize our own personal identity in future post-mortem resurrection experiences. But Hick's new emphasis is still in the process of development, and he surely yet maintains, as he did with his original conception of the eschaton, that one cannot specify its exact nature in advance. He suggests that our present viewpoint is analogous to that of a child who can use the concept of adulthood before this mature condition has been reached.[47] Hick accordingly seems to claim little more than that

> Our eschatological speculation terminates in the idea of the unity of mankind in a state in which the ego-aspect of individual consciousness has been left behind and the relational aspect has developed into a total community which is one-in-many and many-in-one, existing in a state which is probably not embodied and probably not in time.[48]

On the way to this final eschatological state, a person will supposedly experience progressive sanctification and awareness of God, which Hick realizes is not embodied in his original parable of the two travelers. Hick believes that everyone will become increasingly open to and conscious of the divine reality. Confirmation of religious belief will gradually build, as an individual may pass through many new environments of future lives in which the divine goodness will be more fully expressed, until cognitive conclusiveness is finally completely realized in the final eschatological situation.[49]

As noted earlier, Hick believes that cognitive conclusiveness does not occur in this life, because the dissonant circumstances of pain, suffering, wickedness, and ugliness tend to disconfirm belief in the existence of a good God who has kind, loving intentions for his creation. These dissonant circumstances are thought to have been left behind, however, when an individual finally arrives in the eschaton where there will thus be no interference with the full realization of God's kind intentions.[50] Were it not for the presence of evil in the world, Hick is emphatic that the believer would not need further verification of God's reality than may already be warranted by his or her present consciousness of God. The eschatological circumstances, says Hick, will not fundamentally change the believer's cognitive relation to his or her maker. But, thinks Hick,

> this does not render the notion of eschatological verification any less opposite to the function for which it has been advanced—namely establishing the factual character of theistic belief in response to questions raised by contemporary philosophy. It is not that the believer needs further confirmation of his faith, but that the philosopher—whether believer or not—wants to know what aspects of Christian belief bring that system of belief within the accepted criteria of factual meaningfulness.[51]

As we have seen, the problem for the philosopher, according to Hick, is that from our present standpoint within the universe, there is no evidence that decisively shows the truth of statements such as "God created the world" or "God loves mankind." The objective content of our current experience of the universe is not thought to provide the religious person with information by which to specify what would have to occur to prove (or disprove) the love of God or the existence of God.[52] The believer's faith is supposedly confirmed by an interpretive element within his or her religious experience, but this element does not, in Hick's view, have to do with the objective content of the data provided by experience of the material environment.

Philosophers such as F. R. Tennant and Richard Swinburne, however, attempt to use classical a posteriori arguments to prove the existence of God. These philosophers think the objective content of one's experience may in fact provide sufficient grounds for theism, and as I tried to show earlier, Hick seems as yet to be in no position to be sure that they are mistaken. Knowledge claims, in his way of thinking, are relative to each individual. The world may not be religiously ambiguous even though some philosophers think it is.

Pressing my argument further in the next chapter, I will continue to try to show that Hick's system of thought allows both that there may be a possibility of objective evidence for theism in our present world, and that his notion of cognitive conclusiveness regarding the truth of a religious proposition can in principle be achieved through religious experience here and now, assuming Hick has a viable account of religious experience. It will follow, if I am able to show either of these possibilities, that eschatological verification is not essential to Hick's system of thought.

NOTES

[1]John Hick, "Eschatological Verification Reconsidered," *Religious Studies*, Vol. 13, No. 2 (June 1977), p. 192. Others argue just the opposite. Harold I. Brown in *Perception, Theory and Commitment: The New Philosophy of Science* (Chicago: The University of Chicago Press, 1977), has briefly examined the history of logical empiricism, to which Hick is indebted, in order to show that his own Kuhnian approach is superior. Paul

K. Feyerabend, *Against Method* (London: Verso, 1975); Stephen Toulmin, *Foresight and Understanding* (London: Hutchinson's University Library, 1961); Michael Polanyi, *Personal Knowledge* (Chicago: University of Chicago Press, 1958); and others would also take issue with Hick's positivist tendencies, but to consider their views is outside the scope of this study.

[2]Ibid.

[3]John Hick, *Faith and Knowledge* (2nd ed.; Cleveland: Fount Paperbacks, 1978), p. 166.

[4]John Hick, "Eschatological Verification," in *The Logic of God*, ed. by Malcolm Diamond and Thomas Litzenburg, Jr. (Indianapolis: The Bobbs-Merrill Company, Inc., 1975), p. 191.

[5]See, for example, Kai Nielsen, "Eschatological Verification," *Canadian Journal of Theology*, Vol. 4 (1963), pp. 271-281, and Antony Flew, *New Essays in Philosophical Theology* (London: SCM Press, Ltd., 1955), pp. 98-99. A good account of others who argue in this vein is found in William T. Blackstone, *The Problems of Religious Knowledge* (Englewood Cliffs: Prentice-Hall, Inc., 1963), ch. 6. Here Blackstone develops the views of R. M. Hare, J. J. C. Smart, R. F. Holland, Thomas McPherson, R. B. Braithwaite, Ronald Hepburn, and Alasdair MacIntyre.

[6]Hick, "Eschatological Verification Reconsidered," p. 195.

[7]J. L. Mackie, "Evil and Omnipotence," *Mind* (April 1955), p. 200.

[8]Hick, "Eschatological Verification Reconsidered," p. 196.

[9]Hick, *Faith and Knowledge*, p. 118. There is, however, according to Hick, a good possibility some people are partially privy to other minds via mental telepathy. See *Death and Eternal Life* (New York: Harper and Row, Publishers, 1980), p. 42.

[10]Hick, "Eschatological Verification Reconsidered," pp. 200, 193.

[11]John Hick, "Towards a Philosophy of Religious Pluralism," *Neue Zeitschrift fur systematische Theologie*, Vol. 22, No. 2 (1980), p. 143.

[12]John Hick, *God and the Universe of Faiths* (London: The Macmillan Press, Ltd., 1973), p. 100.

[13]Hick, "Towards a Philosophy of Religious Pluralism," p. 147.

[14]Hick, *Death and Eternal Life*, p. 41.

[15]Ibid., p. 50.

[16]Ibid.

[17]Ibid.

[18]Hick, *God and the Universe of Faiths*, p. 42.

[19]Hick, *Faith and Knowledge*, p. 98.

[20]Ibid., p. 101.

[21]Ibid., p. 99.

[22]Ibid.

[23]Ibid., pp. 104-105.

[24]Ibid., p. 104.

[25]John Hick, "On Grading Religions," *Religious Studies*, Vol. 17, No. 4 (1981), p. 457.

[26]Hick, *God and the Universe of Faiths*, p. 40.

[27]Hick, *Death and Eternal Life*, p. 37.

[28]Richard Swinburne, *The Existence of God* (Oxford: Clarendon Press, 1979).

[29]Paul Feyerabend, *Against Method* (London: Verso, 1975), pp. 56-57.

[30]Hick, "Eschatological Verification Reconsidered," p. 193.

[31]Ibid., p. 196.

[32]Ibid.

[33]Ibid.

[34]Ibid.

[35]Ibid., p. 199.

[36]Feyerabend, *Against Method*, p. 56.

[37]Hick, "Eschatological Verification Reconsidered," p. 195.

[38]Ibid.

[39]Ibid.

[40]Ibid.

[41]Works that defend Hick's traditional conception of God are mentioned in note 1 of chapter II. Why is it that Hick is not inclined toward the Whiteheadian view of God is also mentioned there, and I should add that I am in agreement with Hick in this regard.

[42]Hick, "Eschatological Verification Reconsidered," p. 190.

[43]John Hick, *Philosophy of Religion* (2nd ed.; Englewood Cliffs: Prentice-Hall, Inc., 1973), p. 92.

[44]Hick, "Eschatological Verification Reconsidered," p. 202.

[45]Ibid., p. 199.

[46]Hick, "On Grading Religions," p. 462.

[47]Hick, "Eschatological Verification," p. 204.

[48]Hick, *Death and Eternal Life*, p. 464.

[49]Hick, "Eschatological Verification Reconsidered," p. 196. Hick does believe, however, that complete verification could conceivably occur in this present world. He says that the world could change into a "heaven on earth" in which perfected people would live in full God-consciousness (Ibid., p. 201).

[50]Ibid., p. 197.

[51]Hick, *Faith and Knowledge*, p. 194.

[52]Ibid., p. 168.

CHAPTER IV

ESCHATOLOGICAL VERIFICATION RECONSIDERED

In the last chapter, we saw two factors which in Hick's estimation necessitate his notion of eschatological verification. One is that there is supposedly no evidence within the present universe that can decisively either confirm or disconfirm assertions about a loving God. The other is that the circumstances of pain and suffering in the world tend to disconfirm the truth of such theistic statements. Accordingly, Hick predicts a universal eschatological experience that will eventually fully confirm such assertions about God for all humanity. It is proposed that there will be no disconfirming evil circumstances in the future eschatological environment to weigh against everyone's theistic awareness.

In this chapter, I will try to show, however, that neither of the factors that supposedly necessitate eschatological verification does so. First, I will try to show that Hick's argument for there being no possibility of evidence for theism is faulty, thus leaving open the possibility that some evidentialist theistic claims are true, after which, second, we will see that his own system of thought can in principle currently handle the problem of evil without eschatological verification.

1. The Probability of a Religious World View

Hick believes that one comprehensive world view cannot be shown to be superior to another unless arguments are advanced that indicate one is more probable than the other, and

69

unless all parties agree that this is the case.[1] That all parties must agree seems to be inconsistent with the relative nature of human knowledge which we saw implied by Hick's system in the last chapter, but leaving this issue aside for the moment, we should first consider how to compare different world views. Hick points out that

> the criteria by which to match metaphysical systems against each other which have usually been suggested are those developed in connection with the coherence theory of truth—the internal logical consistency of each system of thought; their explanatory comprehensiveness (so that if one covers data which the other has to leave out of account the former is to that extent superior); and the 'adequacy' with which they illuminate and explain what they profess to explain. The first two of these criteria will not help us at this point, since there are forms both of theism and of naturalism which are internally consistent and which are equally comprehensive in the sense that there are no data that evade their explanatory scope. The issue is, once again, not between explanation and no explanation but between two radically different kinds of explanation. The crucial question is thus whether one way of accounting for the data can be said to be inherently more adequate than the other. This is in effect our original problem as to whether theism or naturalism can meaningfully be said to possess a superior antecedent probability. And it now seems that there is no objective sense in which one consistent and comprehensive world view can be described as inherently more probable than another.[2]

Hick's remarks here are directed toward the late F. R. Tennant's attempt (and any other such attempt) to establish the reality of God through philosophical reasoning from the evidences of nature. But Hick's contention is problematic.

Hick seems to beg the question in saying that the first two criteria will not help a thinker such as Tennant. One of the main thrusts of Tennant's work is to show that theism is preferable to naturalism in that it is internally more consistent and comprehensive in coping with the data of the universe. Hick in one place lists the six points of Tennant's argument, which are (1) the mutual adaption of nature and the logico-mathematical capacity of human thought, as well as the richness of thought that may exceed what is needful in nature, (2) the successful, continual adaption of living organisms to their

environment, (3) the fitness of the world on a vast scale to produce and maintain life, (4) a world structure that not only happens to allow living creatures to inhabit it, but also to bear
values and beauty that intelligent beings can appreciate, (5) a
world structure that allows for autonomous rational and ethical life, and (6) the cumulative effect of the last five points
which Tennant thinks call for a theistic explanation.[3] But
after noting these six points, rather than show that naturalism can in fact equally as well account for them, Hick merely
assumes that this is possible.

Hick acknowledges that Tennant developed his argument
after the delayed impact of Hume's "Dialogues" and the acceptance of Darwin's conception of evolution.[4] Yet Hick does
not think that Tennant was successful, not simply because
any one of the items of Tennant's argument may also be interpreted naturalistically, but rather because he depends upon a
comprehensive use of the data to make his case.[5] Attempting
to take into account the entire range of the world's knowable
data, Tennant believed that it is most probable, in terms of a
nonmathematical, alogical concept of probability,[6] that the
world was designed by an intelligent Creator to be a theater
for rational life.[7] Hick's problem with this conclusion is that it
depends upon the entire range of data. He does not believe
that a probability judgment of this sort can be made with a
unique object such as the universe in its entirety. This judgment depends upon what Hick refers to as a total interpretation "...in which we assert that the world as a whole (as experienced by ourselves) is of this or that kind."[8]

A "total interpretation" seems to be our manner of commitment with regard to an over-arching, all-encompassing significance by which we interpret our experience as a whole. Hick
imagines, for example, that he enters a room in a strange
building and stumbles into the meeting of a secret military
society. They mistake him for one of their members, and for
his own safety, he plays the role, hiding his alarm over their
plans to overthrow the constitution. Then Hick suddenly realizes that there are batteries of arc lights and motion picture
cameras behind him in a gallery. He has by accident walked
onto the set of a film being made. The secret society meeting

proceeds, but now Hick interprets the state of affairs to be quite different than he had at first supposed it to be. Similarly, Hick says that the entire physical universe is like a strange room that we enter at birth, in which there "...is no space left for a photographer's gallery, no direction in which we can turn in search of new clues which might reveal the significance of our situation. Our interpretation must be *total* interpretation."[9] Naturalism and theism are examples in Hick's way of thinking of such total interpretations, both equally comprehensive insofar as there are no data that evade their explanatory scope. So neither of these interpretations, thinks Hick, is more or less probable than the other.

Following Hume, Hick says that

> since there is by definition only one universe, all that can be required of an interpretation of it is that account be taken of the entire field of the known data. No *way* of accounting for the data can be said to be, in any objectively ascertainable sense, more probable than another.[10]

Why is one account not more probable than another? "Nothing can be said to be probable per se but only in relation to data beyond itself. And in the special case of our experience as a whole there is nothing beyond itself which could stand in probabilifying relation to it."[11] In saying this, however, I think Hick has stepped outside the bounds of his own system of thought. He is conflating an individual's conceptual awareness of the universe (total though it may be) with the universe itself, even though he ordinarily distinguishes between these.

If, as Hume believed, we live in a world of sense impressions, none of which give rise to the idea of an external world of objects upon which these impressions depend, then it is true that our impressions of the universe stand in relation to nothing else but themselves.[12] But Hick's system of thought is different from Hume's. Hick believes that, although each of us lives in his or her own phenomenal world, there is yet an objective physical reality that gives rise to our consciousness of it. Each individual is thought to have his or her own conceptual awareness of the world, which awareness could be more or less appropriate, because some people have more accurate and extensive information.

Furthermore, a person's total interpretation of the significance of the universe, maximally amplified by taking into account the awareness of every human being that has ever lived, will still nevertheless be limited in the extent to which it actually represents the universe; for the whole of the entire universe could never be completely experienced. Our cognitive machinery, as we saw Hick describe it in the last chapter, is limited in accord with our needs for survival. The process of evolution has left mankind with a limited range of sensitivity by which to preserve and propagate the species. So while Hick is correct in saying that the universe stands in relation to nothing other than itself, the reason he is correct is that this is what we mean by "the universe," even though no one has ever experienced the entire universe. Any individual only has a concept of the universe, a conceptual awareness that stands in a "probabilifying" relation to the continual input of new information. Hick says himself that

> a universal or pancosmic consciousness would...be aware of the entire physical universe as from every perspective at once. This might well be the description of a divine consciousness; but...our separate individuality is constituted precisely by its borders, in virtue of which we are not universally cognitive but know the world within the limitations of a particular perspective, and within this perspective through highly specialized and selective sensory organs.[13]

While the agnostic may thus perceive the universe to be somewhat like a giant vegetating mass that does not reflect any type of purposeful design that is not simply an outgrowth of its own inherent uncreated structure, the theist on the other hand might have a different conception which is both more accurate and more probable in light of the theist's accumulated information. As Hick puts it,

> indeed, the growth of the scientific understanding of the universe has involved continuous evolution of our concepts, as well as occasional theoretical revolutions made possible by the formation of new concepts—and all this in response to the demands of the facts. If we were not willing to face the possibility of conceptual

development and change we should, as a race, have remained at the level of primitive savages. Thus if the universe—in the sense of the range of possible objects of human consciousness—turned out to be more extensive and more complex than our present science assumes, we should I hope be more likely to enlarge our systems of concepts than to close our minds to the facts.[14]

That our system of concepts may be enlarged seems to be inconsistent with the notion of a total interpretation. Rather than there being various total interpretations that are so encompassing they admit of no further clues regarding the significance of our situation, there is always the possibility of new input that might confirm one world view and disconfirm another.

As was mentioned in the last chapter, Hick has said he hopes there is nothing occult in his notion of significance. But we find that, while in some instances "significance" is simply a most general characteristic of our experience that should always be malleable in relation to the world of facts, in other instances Hick talks about awareness of significance as some sort of total interpretation of the universe that is so all-encompassing there can be no new facts admitted. The latter fails to take into account the limited phenomenal character of any one individual's experience of significance that should always be amenable to new input of information from the material environment. A total interpretation seems to have the characteristics of a universal or pancosmic consciousness, the possibility of which Hick's system of thought excludes from the human mind. Since it is excluded, we find that a person's perceived significance of the world (one's world view) may be more or less probable (in a nonmathematical, alogical sense) than the world view of anyone else.

And since Hick's system thus seems to allow one world view to be more or less probable than another, Tennant is therefore in a position to argue that his theistic world view is superior. Tennant's argument seems to entail Hick's notion of complex verifiability, in that the experiential difference in question is spread out over time and variable in the forms it can take. We will not concern ourselves with whether or not Tennant's arguments will work. Although this is a crucial question, it would take us far afield from the present study. Tennant's work simply illustrates that some people think it is possible to specify what would count as evidence for assertions about God. Though I might have used the more recent work of other philosophers such as Richard Swinburne, William Lane Craig, or Richard Taylor,[15] I brought in Tennant because Hick singles him out as having a total interpretation that cannot be evidenced, which argument on Hick's part we have found not to be valid within the context of Hick's system of thought. If Hick is to show that Tennant's theistic explanation of the universe is less desirable than a naturalistic one, he might use the three criteria he mentioned in the quotation near the beginning of this chapter in connection with the coherence theory of truth.

And since Hick is capable of dealing with Tennant via such criteria, the notion of eschatological verification seems to be unnecessary with regard to the theistic language Tennant uses. If the universe in some complex manner provides the possibility of evidence by which to verify talk about God, the prediction of eschatological verification no longer serves a purpose. The kind of evidence Tennant marshals may conceivably be sufficient to render factual status to assertions about God's existence and nature.

Hick might reply with the stipulation, again found at the start of this chapter, that one comprehensive world view is not more probable than another unless all parties agree that it is, which agreement is not possible in the case of a theistic world view. The suggestion that there must be unanimous agreement, however, is inconsistent with the bulk of Hick's thinking. Unanimity of agreement may be impossible in complex situations in view of the relativism in Hick's position that was discussed in the last chapter.

In writing about the nature of knowledge in general, Hick in fact consistently emphasizes a subjective aspect. Following A. J. Ayer, Hick says that there are three conditions for knowing that something is the case. First, what one claims to know must be true. Hick then hastens to distinguish between the logical certainty that he thinks is required by a definition of knowledge, and the psychological limitations of any claim of certitude. Hick explains that, although there can only be knowledge of p when p is true, "...a claim to know p is justified by rational certainty that p, even if it should subsequently become clear that p was not true."[16] Hick is saying that knowledge by definition cannot be erroneous, but that a person's knowledge claim may nevertheless be erroneous despite this person's belief in its truth.

Continuing to stress the psychological limitations of knowledge, a second condition is that we must be sure of what we claim to know, and third, we should have the right to be sure. Expanding upon these last two conditions, Hick says that while knowing something about reality involves the psychological state of an unqualified feeling of certainty, Hick thinks that certitude requires adequate rational grounds. It must be arrived at self-critically and judiciously. When we say we "know" something with certainty, we are not referring to a casual absence of doubt but to knowledge that has withstood critical scrutiny. Hick does not believe it is "...possible to specify the exact amount of criticism necessary to constitute rational certainty."[17] Yet he maintains that we sometimes reach a point in our cognitive procedures where we are intellectually satisfied and feel confident that we have grasped the truth of some specific proposition. This dogmatic sense of finality carries the important rider, says Hick, that what is in this way evident to us can be evident to others as well. We are assured that we are justified in being rationally certain of the truth of a proposition when we feel that anyone else confronted with the same evidence can likewise be certain of it. So despite the subjective aspect of knowledge, there is also an objective character. "It is objective in the sense that it is 'the same for everyone.' That which I know is in principle knowable by others."[18]

Passing over questions that might be raised, I will only point out that in so conceiving the conditions of knowledge,[19] Hick has not in any way discounted the claims of thinkers such as Tennant and Swinburne. For they no doubt feel they have grasped the truth of the propositions of their respective world view by way of experiential grounds that justify their beliefs, and they surely also think that what they know is in principle knowable by others, that is, that others confronted with the same evidence should similarly be led to the same conclusion.

It seems then that Hick has no apparent justification for excluding the possibility of one world view being more or less nonmathematically probable than another. Having shown this does not in any way entail that there is in fact evidence for a theistic world view, but we have at least found that Hick's means of discounting the claims of some who think there is evidence for theism will not work. Given Hick's conditions of factual meaning and the general characteristics of the verifying experience examined in the previous chapter, it seems that as long as those who make assertions about the presence and purpose of God can specify what in principle counts as verification of these assertions, these people are then entitled to consider their assertions factual. Assuming that thinkers like Tennant and Swinburne probably have thus, in Hick's way of thinking, sufficiently indicated a means of complex verification that is conceptually possible, their theistic language should be considered factual unless Hick can show otherwise, the problem of evil notwithstanding.

Tennant and Swinburne have each developed a theodicy by which to defend the goodness of God.[20] Were they successful in their effort (and if their other arguments were correct), then, contrary to Hick's view, assertions about the presence and purpose of a benevolent God could be confirmed for individuals despite the problem of evil. But there is no need to pursue this possibility. In the next section of this chapter, we will see that even Hick's theodicy can in principle account for the existence of evil, and Hick's theodicy could be incorporated into either Tennant's or Swinburne's thinking, were it somehow found that their own theodicies will not suffice. I say "somehow found" because of the relativism in Hick's system of thought. If a person claims to have a theodicy with which he or she is satisfied, it would be difficult for Hick to show that this theodicy is mistaken, as we will see in considering Hick's views on the problem of evil.

2. Evil and the God of Love

We have seen Hick argue that complete conclusive confirmation of assertions about the presence and purpose of God is not possible. Although a person's religious experience may be sufficiently vivid that one who has had such a powerful sense of the divine presence must claim to know that God is real, Hick yet thinks that the circumstances of pain and suffering in the world tend to disconfirm the possibility of a benevolent creator. Hence, doubt concerning the truth of assertions about the existence of a divine being cannot supposedly currently be completely removed from a rational observer's mind, for people tend to think that an omnipotent, loving God would not permit such circumstances. Hick nevertheless predicts a future eschatological situation in which there will be complete confirmation of such theistic statements, because there will then supposedly be no disconfirming circumstances of pain and suffering. Such statements are thus in principle verifiable eschatologically, and it is thought that they should therefore be treated as factual assertions at present.

Eschatological verification is then an unnecessary doctrine if it can be shown that evil circumstances are compatible with Hick's conception of deity, that is, if it is plausible to predict the possibility of currently experiencing these evil circumstances in accord with Hick's description of a loving God. This is not to say that Hick actually has a solution to the problem of evil, for in showing that one's awareness of God can conceivably be congruent with the world's evils, I will assume the truth of both Hick's theodicy and his account of religious experience, even though these assumptions are not warranted outside the context of the argument in the present chapter. In the next chapter, we will find that he does not have an acceptable account of religious experience and that he therefore also does not have sufficient means to advance either his theodicy or many of the other religious claims he takes to be factual. With the importance of Hick's account of religious experience thus in view, we will proceed now to consider it in detail after we have first had a brief look at his theodicy in his own words.

As we saw in the first chapter, Hick believes our present

world environment was created by God as the first phase of our spiritual development or soul-making.

> Its successive events, both good and evil, have not been individually "sent" by God, nor planned as a divinely prearranged obstacle course. What is divinely created is a world, functioning in accordance with its own laws, in which human freedom is exercised with real consequences in response to real problems and challenges. That life's contingencies, including both its blessings and its calamities, affect us indiscriminately, and not in proportion to our desert, is a precondition of the moral life and hence of the moral growth of a person. For if bad things happened always and only to evil people, and good things only to good people, we should inevitably be seeking rewards and avoiding penalties rather than making genuine moral choices....All...our world, with its ambiguities and mysteries, its evils as well as the good within it, may be a phase in the outworking of a creative divine purpose which is leading us to limitless good. And if our awareness of God as good and loving is strong enough to bear the weight, we are, I believe, entitled to opt for this interpretation of human existence.[21]

More of the workings of this theodicy will be brought in later. First we should consider that in which awareness of God is thought to consist, since it is this awareness that enables the theist to cope with experiences of evil. As noted earlier, the believer's awareness of God is described in terms of experiencing-as, which is synonymous with Hick's understanding of religious faith in its primary sense. To develop this concept of faith, Hick depends upon an adaption of Wittgenstein's discussion of ordinary visual experiences referred to as seeing-as in the *Philosophical Investigations.*[22]

There Wittgenstein used ambiguous puzzle pictures and diagrams such as Jostrow's duck-rabbit as illustrations of things that can appear to an observer in various ways. The duck-rabbit drawing may appear as either a duck or a rabbit or both simultaneously. Accordingly, says Hick, "we speak of seeing-as when that which is objectively there, in the sense of that which affects the retina, can be consciously perceived in two different ways as having two different characters or natures or meanings or significances; and," Hick continues, "very often, in these two-dimensional instances, we find that the mind switches back and forth between the alternative ways of seeing-as."[23]

Hick then expands this notion of seeing-as into that of experiencing-as, which includes in addition to seeing, the different sensations of hearing, feeling, tasting, and smelling that normally cooperate with seeing as our means of perception. This is to move up a step from two-dimensional pictures and diagrams to real life. We may experience an object in a field as either a rabbit or a tuft of grass. Or, experiencing-as, we may perceive a piece of limestone to be either an artifact or a rock. But Hick does not mean to be suggesting that experiencing-as is an atypical instance of perception.

All experience should be construed as experiencing-as. Hick thinks for example that a familiar object, such as a fork, might be recognized by a Stone-Age savage "...as a marvelously shining object which must be full of mana and must not be touched; or as a small but deadly weapon; or as a tool for digging; or just as something utterly baffling and unidentifiable."[24] That we are able to identify forks is the result of their being a familiar part of the apparatus of our culture. The meaning of an artifact is not stamped upon it, but is rather determined within a particular cultural context by the purpose for which it was made.

> We have learned, starting from scratch, to identify rabbits and forks and innumerable other kinds of things. And so there is thus far in principle no difficulty about the claim that we may learn to use the concept 'act of God' as we have learned to use other concepts, and acquire the capacity to recognize exemplifying instances.[25]

Hick admits that there is considerable contrast between such concepts as rabbit and fork and the concept of a divine act. Rabbits and forks are objects, whereas a divine act, says Hick, is an event. Enlarging the contrast still further, Hick maintains that

> ...the cognition of God recorded in the Bible is much wider in scope than an awareness of particular isolated events as being acts of God. Such divine acts are but points of peculiarly intense focus within a much wider awareness of existing in the presence of God.

Indeed the biblical cognition of God is typically mediated through the whole experience of the prophet or apostle after his call or conversion, even though within this totality there are specially vivid moments of awareness of God, some of which are evoked by striking or numinous events which thereby become miracles or theophanies.[26]

But while a sense of living within the ambiance of the unseen God is far removed from the recognition of forks and rabbits, there are, according to Hick, connecting links by which the religious awareness can become intelligible to us. In investigating this continuity between religious and secular experience, Hick suggests that experiencing-as occurs at various levels. Hick means

> ...that as well as there being values of x and y such that to experience A as x is incompatible with experiencing it as y, because x and y are mutually exclusive alternatives, there are also values x and y such that it is possible to experience A as simultaneously x and y. Here y is supplementary to x, but on a different level. What is meant by 'levels' in this context? That y is on a higher level than x means that the experiencing of A as y presupposes but goes beyond the experiencing of it as x.[27]

An example of x and y being mutually exclusive is the fact that one cannot see a tuft of grass simultaneously as both a tuft of grass and as a rabbit, or a piece of paper could not be experienced as both a piece of paper and an ink spill simultaneously. But an example of y as supplementary to x can be seen in the experience of a car going through the motions required by a stop sign. One may see what is approaching the stop sign as a car; or it may be seen as a Chevy that trails smoke; or it may be seen as a Chevy that needs a set of intake valve guide seals. Each of these later recognitions is on a successively higher level in that each presupposes and goes beyond the previous one. As we saw earlier in this chapter, Hick understands these various levels of recognition in terms of awareness of significance, in that significance is the correlate of experiencing-as, and he thinks that the significance of any given situation may be characterized according to three different levels. These are the natural, the ethical, and the religious.[28]

Natural significance is that of the physical world or the objective environment to whose character we must continually relate ourselves if we are to survive.

The level of moral or ethical significance is related to the natural order. "This ethical experience is an order of significance that supervenes upon, interpenetrates and is mediated through the physical significance which it presupposes."[29] On those occasions when the moral character of a situation is not readily apparent to us, yet comes to us as we contemplate it, what is happening, thinks Hick, is comparable to our discovery of a pattern emerging from a puzzle picture. Much as the same lines and marks that we have seen as a rabbit come to constitute the new picture of a duck, "...so the social situation is there with the same physically significant features. But we have now come to be aware of it as laying upon us an inescapable moral claim."[30]

Transcending ethical awareness is what Hick believes to be the third and higher level of significance. The "...more ultimately fateful momentous matter of relating ourselves to the divine, to God, is not distinct from the task of directing ourselves within the natural and ethical spheres; on the contrary, it entails (without being reducible to) a way of so directing ourselves."[31] It is a level of significance that adds a dimension that both includes and transcends the level of moral judgment, though it does not simply continue the pattern that Hick has already suggested. It is more complex. Hick thinks that it is safe to say that every instance of ethical significance presupposes a natural level of significance, because there can be no moral situation if there is no physical situation to occasion it. But the nature of religious awareness is not always superimposed upon an occasion of moral obligation. One may be conscious of God while he or she is in solitude, without any sense of moral requirement. And while religious awareness may involve a specific environmental context involving the wonder and beauty of nature, it may as well be relatively independent of external circumstances when one is wrapped in contemplative and mystical awareness through prayer or meditation. Hick wants to maintain, nevertheless, that even when one has religious experience in solitude, it normally directs us toward other people and deepens the ethical significance of our relations with them.

For the purpose of examining the need for eschatological verification, we will only be concerned with the natural and religious levels of experience. Assuming Hick's theodicy and his account of religious experience are correct, we may experience the events of our lives and of human history as either purely natural events or as mediating the presence and activity of a loving God, sometimes even when the natural events produce pain and suffering. We have seen the Hebrew prophet Jeremiah used as such an example. Hick seems to think that Jeremiah was able to experience the Chaldean attack upon Jerusalem as the judgment of God, while a reading of Jeremiah indicates that the prophet also experienced God to be loving.[32] It thus appears that natural circumstances involving evil can be identified with the purpose of a benevolent God. Hick clearly seems to believe that some rational people maintain an awareness of God despite their experiences of suffering and evil. Tragedy in these cases may become a further stage in the realization of God's loving purpose. These people respond to circumstances of challenge and temptation by accepting adversity, pain, and affliction in order to bring these circumstances into the sphere of the divine purpose. They are able to recognize or interpret these circumstances as part of God's plan. The crucifixion of Christ, for instance, was the greatest of all evils, but because of Christ's response, Hick says it was made the occasion of human redemption.[33] So even the worst of evils can be recognized to be compatible with the divine presence and purpose in this present earthly existence. An individual's perception of the significance of God's purpose and plan for mankind must enable a person to put the circumstances of pain and suffering in their divine perspective.

Evil is thus recognized to serve God's good purposes, and it is the interpretative element in Hick's account of experience that seems to allow rational people to understand evil in this way. But while Hick's system of thought allows this sort of interpretation of evil, he does not seem to think that the resulting awareness of evil as an instrument for God's good purposes is sufficient in some cases to remove rational doubt concerning the truth of propositions about God.[34] Hick apparently does not believe that the interpretive element in the experience of objects and events will satisfy those individuals who are deeply engulfed in personal tragedy.[35] But I believe this is at least an oversight on Hick's part. For as we saw in the case of Jeremiah, Hick often indicates that individuals such as the writers of Scripture are capable of experiencing pain and suffering in accord with theistic belief. It seems, moreover, that Hick's view entails that it is logically possible that this could be the case no matter what the degree of pain and grief experienced, as is evidenced by Scripture.

The writing of Scripture, in Hick's view, is the result of a person's faith in the divine reality. By "faith," we saw that Hick means that voluntary interpretive act by which people become aware of God through ordinary objects and events. Faith is a human response to God's self-revelation in the history of the world which becomes actual through a person's religious experiencing-as. Hick believes this experience makes possible an uncompelled cognition of the presence and purpose of God while preserving the freedom and responsibility of the individual in relation to God's infinite, omnipotent nature.[36] Knowledge of the presence and purpose of God is in this way supposedly revealed to people in this life. Conceivably, therefore, any rational person could acquire (as did the prophets and apostles) an awareness of God's loving purpose with regard to any set of this-worldly circumstances. Presuming this is possible, eschatological verification is then not necessary to establish theistic statements as factual, for one could experience the circumstances of the world, including its evils, in conjunction with the presence and purpose of God. This sort of comprehensive theistic recognition of the world's circumstances would provide the experiential difference by which to verify religious propositions. A person involved in this sort of recognitional response could presumably even record his or her experiences, and as a result, in Hick's view, would have produced Scripture.

The recording of such religious experiences may also become revelatory in a secondary sense. Scripture is an account of revelatory events that became revelatory through the faith of its writers, and Hick believes it in turn may mediate the same revelation to people of subsequent generations who have a response of faith to it.[37] Portions of the Bible such as the book of Job, the Psalms and the Prophets, and the epistles of Peter, Paul, and James are early records of the perception of the significance of pain and suffering as a means of God's love and care. James, for instance, writes, "Count is all joy, my brethren, when you meet various trials, for you know that the testing of your faith produces steadfastness. And let steadfastness have its full effect, that you may be perfect and complete, lacking in nothing."[38] One could also turn to the writings of Job to find specific instances of nearly any kind of pain and suffering that God might discriminantly allow to befall those individuals who are being perfected. Such instances, according to philosophers such as Marilyn Adams, can be interpreted to be reflective of God's love in the following ways.[39]

Through times of testing the believer is made to examine whether he or she loves God more than the temporal goods that are being extracted, and as a result, the believer's relationship with God may be deepened. Adams points out that the Bible is full of such stories. God promised to multiply Abraham's descendants. Then Abraham is tested by being called to leave his homeland,[40] and later again tested by being asked to sacrifice his son.[41] In coming to love God more than any temporal good, and in being able to trust God to see to his or her good even in the face of death, the believer becomes rightly related to and aware of God.[42]

Adams argues further that, when God allows a person to be persecuted (always within the limits of what this person can bear), "...the martyr's sacrifice can be used as an instrument of divine judgment, because it draws the persecutor an external picture of what he is really like—the more innocent the victim, the clearer the focus."[43] Adams says the paradigm case of this type of divine judgment is found in the relationship of Jesus to the Sadducees and Pharisees. These men did not acknowledge their need for God, and they held others in contempt. In allowing Himself to be crucified by them, Jesus permitted "...their sinful attitudes to be carried into action and externalized in His own flesh. Because He is a truly innocent victim, His Body

85

is the canvas on which the portrait of their sins can be most clearly drawn."[44]

Adams thinks God's motive for using martyrdom as a vehicle of divine judgment is the hope of reconciliation. Those who are not too hard-hearted may repent and experience redemption after recognizing their sins. When Christians find themselves suffering at the hands of others, they may thus be grateful to God for counting them worthy to share in the work to reconcile the world through loving kindness.[45]

It seems plausible, then, that a person may have a direct theistic recognition of the evil circumstances of the world as is exemplified by the writers of Scripture, or one may respond in faith indirectly to such circumstances through Scriptures that have already been written. Such an experience (whether direct or indirect through faith in Scripture) could conceivably equip a rational person with an interpretive framework by which to cope with any painful set of circumstances that might be encountered. Like Job, this person could be aware of the presence and purpose of God despite the loss of everything including life itself. Though perhaps only a child, this person could say of God, "Though he slay me, yet will I trust in him."[46] The circumstances of pain and suffering would thus no longer disconfirm this person's faith. This person could in principle reach the point of complete conclusiveness with regard to the confirmation of his or her religious convictions, which point would in Hick's way of thinking constitute verification of them. And since this person's level of awareness could in principle be attained by any rational observer, it should be this possibility, and not necessarily the concept of eschatological verification, that renders factual status to assertions about God's presence and purpose. For if verification can in principle occur here and now, there is then no need to look for a situation that might provide verification in the future. The imagined eschatological situation is unnecessary.

The plausibility of either Hick's theodicy or his account of religious experience does not concern us. I happen to believe that they are both problematic, but a discussion of my reasons for thinking this would distract from my purpose here.[47] I am trying to show that while the truth of assertions about the presence and purpose of a loving God may currently be doubted (the conditions of the world seem to indicate to many people that they are false), it is yet possible in Hick's way of thinking to imagine a sustained experience of the world that would exclude any such grounds for rational doubt of the truth of these theistic assertions. Assuming, as Hick would have it, that verification of such theistic assertions is a complex matter, it seems that the cumulative effect of a sustained theistic experience could in principle lead to their verification.

It does not matter how harsh and painful the evil circumstances might be. Volcanic eruptions and earthquakes may kill thousands of terrified people, dreaded diseases such as leukemia may take the lives of innocent children, there may be holocausts, and so forth. In any event, Hick believes that a world such as ours in which these evils occur "...may be a phase in the outworking of a creative divine purpose which is leading us to limitless good. And if our awareness of God as good and loving is strong enough to bear the weight, we are, I believe," says Hick, "entitled to opt for this interpretation of human existence."[48] It is thus not only logically possible, it is also plausible, in Hick's way of thinking, for a rational person to experience evil circumstances as compatible with the purposes of a loving creator of the universe.

How exactly this theistic experience might be brought about in an individual's awareness is a mystery, according to Hick. But he insists that "we may learn to use the concept 'act of God,' as we have learned to use other concepts, and acquire the capacity to recognize exemplifying instances."[49] It seems then that it is logically possible, according to Hick's system, that any instance of evil, however horrendous, could be seen as not inconsistent with God's good purposes. If Jeremiah can see the Chaldeans' attack upon Israel as an activity of God, other instances involving evil might be interpreted theistically as well, as is implied by Hick's statement that "for a few the eschaton has already been realized in the present."[50] To realize the eschaton at present, one must be fully God-conscious,[51] which consciousness, says Hick, includes seeing all of life's "...requirements, disciplines, mercies, rebukes, and joys as mediating the divine presence."[52] This person will realize that, despite all of life's rough edges, "In everything God works for good with those who love him."[53]

Hick might complicate the issue by arguing that even if the positive value of pain and suffering could somehow presently be recognized by people as a part of God's soul-making program, the plurality of the various world religions seems to have an even greater doubt-instilling effect upon the recognition of the divine presence and purpose. Only by way of eschatological verification, he might argue, will we be able to treat the divergent claims of the many religious systems as factual claims, especially as these claims have to do with the various means of salvation which he says will eventually somehow apply to all humankind. For example, he states that

> ...what Christians call the Mystical Body of Christ within the life of God, and Hindus the universal Atman which we are, and Mahayana Buddhists the self-transcending unity in the Dharma Body of the Buddha, consists of the wholeness of ultimately perfected humanity beyond the existence of separate egos.[54]

Such a statement could hardly be known to be true now. How could we know this side of the eschaton whether the Body of Christ, the universal Atman, and the Dharma Body of the Buddha, each consists of or refers to the same thing? The Christian, Buddhist, Hindu, and Moslem each seem to have a different form of religious experience and belief, which Hick believes will ultimately be verified or falsified eschatologically. In Islam, in one type of Judaism, and maybe in one type of Buddhism, the universe is predicted to have a certain definite fulfillment, the post-mortem occurrence of which will leave us beyond rational doubt concerning the veracity of these predictions.[55] We will find as a result of this fulfillment, thinks Hick, that many of the various major religious faiths are sufficient to lead humanity to God.

But from where does Hick's faith in universalism and the plurality of religions come? Hick seems to feel justified in holding these beliefs. If so, why should we not understand this justification by way of his doctrine of experiencing-as? Unless Hick or others upon whom he relies have had a level of religious awareness in which the significance of the various religions were perceived to be compatible, he surely would not promote the plurality of religions. And it seems to me that such an awareness could be obtained were Hick's religious hypotheses correct.

Assuming, as Hick does, that the Vedas and Upanishades of Hinduism, the Koran of Islam, the Granth of Sikhism, and so on are each forms of revelation,[56] then eschatological verification is obviously not necessary to establish statements about the core beliefs of these faiths as factual. Revelation, as we have seen, is itself the result of an experience or recognitional response that seems to remove doubt about the truth of some religious assertions. Since anyone could in principle have an experience of Scripture as revelatory, those propositions that would be verified by this experience should be considered factual, and as we have seen Hick is already doing, they might be compared with regard to the possibility of universal salvation.

The naturalist would obviously accept little of this. In accord with the line of reasoning mentioned earlier, the naturalist would perhaps think that if there were a good omnipotent self-revealingly active God, there would be no evil nor plurality of world religions. But that the naturalist might think something like this does not exclude the logical possibility that he or she may some day come to interpret the universe as mediating the presence and purpose of God. There may even be God-conscious people of one religion or another who choose not to interpret evil circumstances as a means for soulmaking, but their decision would not affect the possibility that, according to Hick's concept of experiencing-as, they could so choose if they wanted. In principle, Hick's system of thought seems plausibly to entail that any rational person could choose to realize that pain and suffering or any other set of this-worldly religious circumstances make a positive contribution to the process of the making of our souls.[57] I conclude, therefore, that eschatological verification is not an essential element of Hick's system of thought.

This conclusion, of course, depends upon the veracity of Hick's concept of religious experience. If it is possible for anyone to experience the world's evils in conjunction with the presence and purpose of God, so that cognitive conclusiveness of the truth of theistic propositions can in principle be obtained in this life, then there is no need to predict the occurrence of these circumstances in a future eschaton. If Hick's concept of religious experience is not veridical, however, then there is still no need for eschatological verification. For Hick's account of Scriptural revelation, which predicts an eschaton, is merely a written record of religious experience. Without a workable concept of religious experience, Hick thus has no basis for his eschatological predictions. There would be little more reason to predict a future eschaton than there is for predicting the existence of griffins and mermaids. So, on the one hand, if Hick has a viable concept of religious experience, there is then no need for eschatological verification, while on the other hand, if he does not have a viable concept of religious experience, then he has no cause for eschatological verification.[58] Whether or not Hick's concept of religious experience is in fact veridical is the topic of the next chapter.

NOTES

[1]John Hick, *Arguments for the Existence of God* (New York: The Seabury Press, 1971), p. 21, and his *The Existence of God* (New York: The Macmillan Company, 1964), p. 12.

[2]Hick, *Arguments for the Existence of God*, pp. 32-33.

[3]F.R. Tennant, *Philosophical Theology*, Vol. II, *The World, The Soul, and God* (Cambridge: The University Press, 1956), ch. 4.

[4]Hick, *Arguments for the Existence of God*, p. 18, and Tennant, *Philosophical Theology*, Vol. II, p. 112.

[5]Tennant also believed that the items of his argument for the existence of God, taken separately, might be interpreted naturalistically (see *Philosophical Theology*, Vol. II, p. 79). He may have gone too far in suggesting this possibility, however, and it seems to me that this suggestion does not give Hick license to assume the possibility of a naturalist interpretation. Hick might at least evaluate some of the attempts to account for the universe naturalistically, such as is done in Jacques Monod's *Chance and Necessity* (New York: Vintage Books, 1971), or Louis Althusser's and Etienne Balibar's *Reading Capital* (New York: Schocken Books, 1979).

[6]Tennant, *Philosophical Theology*, Vol. I, p. 283, and Vol. II, p. 88.

[7]Ibid., Vol. 11, p. 105.

[8]John Hick, *Faith and Knowledge* (2nd ed.; Cleveland: Fount Paperbacks, 1978), p. 114. For an obscure attempt to criticize Hick's notion of a total interpretation, see Kirk Wilson, "John Hick on Total Interpretation," *The New Scholastic*, Vol. 52 (1978), pp. 280-284.

[9]Ibid.

[10]Ibid., p. 154.

[11]Ibid., p. 152. Hick uses this same argument in *Arguments for the Existence of God*, pp. 13-14, 28-33; *Philosophy of Religion* (Englewood Cliffs: Prentice-Hall, Inc., 1973), pp. 26-28; and *The Existence of God*, pp. 11-12. Hick mentions in these places that there are various types of probability theories that are each inappropriate in determining the character of the universe for the reason we have seen. The type of probability that I will attribute to theoreticians such as Tennant and Swinburne is a nonmathematical one that does not require assigning numerical values to objects and events.

[12]David Hume, *A Treatise of Human Nature*, ed. by L. A. Selby-Bigge (Oxford: The Clarendon Press, 1960), p. 189.

[13]John Hick, *Death and Eternal Life* (New York: Harper and Row, Publishers, 1980), p. 233.

[14]Ibid., p. 287.

[15]Richard Swinburne, *The Existence of God* (Oxford: The Clarendon Press, 1979); William Lane Craig, *The Kalam Cosmological Argument* (London: The Macmillan Press, 1979); Richard Taylor, *Metaphysics* (2nd ed.; Englewood Cliffs: Prentice-Hall, Inc., 1974).

[16]Hick, *Faith and Knowledge*, p. 208.

[17]Ibid., p. 207.

[18]Ibid.

[19]For an example of such questions, see Carl Reinhold Brakenhielm's analysis of Hick's views in *How Philosophy Shapes Theories of Religion* (Lund: C. W. I. Gleerup, 1975), pp. 75-81.

[20]Tennant, *Philosophical Theology*, Vol. II, pp. 180-181; Swinburne, *The Existence of God*, pp. 200-224.

[21]Stephen T. Davis, ed., *Encountering Evil* (Atlanta: John Knox Press, 1981), pp. 64-65.

[22]Wittgenstein, *Philosophical Investigations*, Pt. 11, sec. xi.

[23]John Hick, *God and the Universe of Faiths* (Glasgow: Fount Paperbacks, 1977), p. 39.

[24]Ibid., p. 41.

[25]Ibid., p. 44.

[26]Ibid.

[27]Ibid., pp. 44-45.

[28]Ibid.

[29]Ibid., p. 46.

[30]Ibid., pp. 46-47.

[31]Hick, *Faith and Knowledge*, p. 107.

[32]Jeremiah 9:24, 31:3.

[33]Hick, *Faith and Knowledge*, p. 233, and *Philosophy of Religion*, p. 42.

[34]John Hick, "Eschatological Verification Reconsidered," *Religious Studies*, Vol. 13, No. 2 (June 1977), p. 196.

[35]John Hick, *Evil and the God of Love* (New York: Harper and Row, Publishers, 1978), p. 386.

[36]Hick, *God and the Universe of Faiths*, pp. 50-51.

[37]Ibid.

[38]James 1:2, 18 (Revised Standard Version).

[39]Marilyn McCord Adams, "Martyrdom: A Christian Solution to the Problem of Evil," (unpublished paper presented at the Second Annual Pacific Regional Conference for the Society of Christian Philosophers, Westmont College, Santa Barbara, California, March, 1982), p. 12.

[40]Genesis 12.

[41]Genesis 22.

[42]Adams, "Martyrdom: A Christian Solution to the Problem of Evil," pp. 8-11.

[43]Ibid., p. 10.

[44]Ibid., p. 11.

[45]Ibid., p. 16.

[46]Job 13:15.

[47]For a critical appraisal of Hick's view of religious experience, see Bryant Keeling and Mario Morelli, "Beyond Wittgensteinian Fideism: An Examination of John Hick's Analysis of Religious Faith," *International Journal for Philosophy of Religion*, Vol. 8 (1977), pp. 250-262, and James Heaney, "Faith and the Logic of Seeing-as," *International Journal for the Philosophy of Religion*, Vol. 10 (1979), pp. 189-198. For a critical appraisal of Hick's theodicy, see Davis, *Encountering Evil*, pp. 53-63. Though not directed specifically toward Hick, another good analysis of one of the more crucial problems with which Hick's theodicy must cope (justification of the amount of suffering in the world) is found in William L. Rowe, "The Problem of Evil and Some Varieties of Atheism," *American Philosophical Quarterly*, Vol. 16, No. 4 (October, 1979) pp. 335-341. On the other hand, works that support a theodicy such as Hick's include Davis, *Encountering Evil*, pp. 69-83, 92-99, Alvin Plantinga, *God, Freedom, and Evil* (New York: Harper and Row, Publishers, 1974), and C. S. Lewis, *The Problem of Pain* (New York: The Macmillian Company, 1944).

[48]John Hick, "Hick's Response to Critiques," in *Encountering Evil*, ed. by Davis, p. 65.

[49]Hick, *God and the Universe of Faiths*, p. 44.

[50]John Hick, "On Grading Religions," *Religious Studies*, Vol. 17, No. 4 (1981), p. 462.

[51]Hick, "Eschatological Verification Reconsidered," p. 196.

[52]Hick, *Faith and Knowledge*, p. 215.

[53]Romans 8:28 as quoted by Hick in *Faith and Knowledge*, p. 259.

[54]Hick, *Death and Eternal Life*, p. 464.

[55]Hick, *Arguments for the Existence of God*, p. 118.

[56]Hick, *Death and Eternal Life*, p. 325.

[57]Hick of course admits there are logically possible situations that would render theistic language factual. As he says, for example, "The world could conceivably change into a 'heaven on earth' in which perfect human beings live in full God-consciousness unimpeded by any jarring circumstances" ("Eschatological Verification Reconsidered," p. 201). But Hick goes on to say that he does not think this possibility is plausible in light of theistic traditions which look for perfection in the future eschaton. My conclusion is plausible in light of Hick's system of thought, if not also often in light of mainstream theistic tradition.

[58]There have been numerous other criticisms of Hick's notion of eschatological verification that tend to fall into one of two classifications. In chapter II we looked at those which reject verification requirements and therefore also reject the need for eschatological verification. Plantinga and Mavrodes take this approach. Of the other class which tends to be sympathetic to verificationism, some have argued that the notion of surviving bodily destruction is incoherent, and some have contended that Hick does not give a sufficient account of the conditions under which one would be justified in saying that he or she survived death, and so on. My own interest is removed from either of these two classifications of objection. I am primarily trying to show that eschatological verification is not an essential element of Hick's system of thought. Whether or not his concept of eschatological verification will actually provide some religious statements with factual assertion status need not concern us, and thus I will not entertain the various arguments that suggest it may not provide this status. For a list of sources that do criticize Hick in this way, see his article, "Eschatological Verification Reconsidered," p. 191.

CHAPTER V

THE RATIONALITY OF RELIGIOUS BELIEF

In the previous chapter we found that if Hick's account of religious experience is veridical, there is then no need for his notion of eschatological verification. In this chapter, I will follow through and look at Hick's argument for the rationality or veracity of religious experience. We will find that his argument does not work because it depends upon an analogy that does not hold. He thinks that just as it is rational to interpret our ordinary phenomenal awareness as though it has to do with a material environment (over against the possibility of a solipsist alternative), it is similarly rational for people to interpret their theistic awareness as having to do with God (over against the possibility of denial of a divine noumenal reality). But the supposed solipsist alternative will be found to rest upon the assumption that we are kept from contact with the material environment by sense data, which assumption I shall suggest is unwarranted unless Hick were somehow to show that his use of the concept of sense data is acceptable. We will further see that there is a great deal of dissimilarity between ordinary and religious types of experience, and in emphasizing these dissimilarities, we will find that Hick's understanding of religious experience is not supportive of his own theistic claims. I will conclude, then, that unless Hick can (1) account for the differences between ordinary and religious types of experiences, and (2) substantiate his view of the role of sense data, he has no basis for believing that his account of religious experience is veridical. Implied by this conclusion is then that Hick has insufficient grounds for advocating the notion of eschatological verification. We will begin with Hick's argument for the rationality of religious belief.

1. A Bad Analogy

According to Hick, there is a basic act of interpretation (apparently not a total interpretation as discussed in the previous chapter) that reveals to us the actual existence of the material world. It is this primary interpretive act that carries us beyond the solipsist predicament into an objective world that we share with other people. This interpretive bias by which we are prevented from falling into solipsism is not supported by evidence except for what Hick calls the permissive evidence of one's phenomenal experience that is simply "...'there' to be interpreted either solipsistically or otherwise."[1] The solipsist's hypothesis represents an alternative and rival interpretation to the contrary belief in a plurality of minds that exist in a common world, and "...there is no event within our phenomenal experience the occurrence or non-occurrence of which is relevant to the truth or falsity of the solipsist hypothesis."[2]

Hick thinks that it may be objected that if it does not make any practical difference whether or not solipsism is true, there might not be two different interpretations of our experience. Our experience considered phenomenologically would be the same on either account. But Hick does not think that this objection holds. If the solipsist interpretation were to be seriously adopted, the difference made by genuinely assenting to solipsism would be akin to the sudden realization while dreaming that one was in fact dreaming. "Our personal relationships in particular, our loves and friendships, our hates and enmities, rivalries and cooperations, would have to be treated not as trans-subjective meetings with other personalities, but as dialogues and dramas within oneself."[3] There would be an unreal character in contrast with one's former non-solipsist mode of experience. People who adopt the solipsist alternative should thus be considered insane. Their insanity would consist in the fact that they would no longer regard other people as independent centers of consciousness with a will and purpose of their own. They would be living in a one-person world.[4]

Even though the sanely functioning mind cannot seriously assent to it, solipsism is, according to Hick, as much a logically possible interpretation of experience as that of an external world which we ordinarily hold. "It follows that our normal mode of experience is itself properly described as an interpretation, an interpretation which we are unable to justify by argument but which we have nevertheless no inclination or reason to doubt."[5]

But Hick's argument here is weak in that he has assumed that we do not have contact with the world. We only have contact with sensory information that somehow constitutes our phenomenal awareness, the significance of which is furthermore an interpretation. Hick says we

> normally experience our sensory impressions in terms of a three-dimensional world of objects in space around us. But that there is, at least in principle, something optional about this is shown by the fact that if someone believed that only his own consciousness existed and that the whole course of his experience was analogous to a dream, you could not dislodge him from this 'solipsism' (as it is called) by any logical argument. This does not indicate that our normal interpretation of our sense experience is doubtful, but that despite its indubitable character it is nevertheless an interpretation of data which are capable of being interpreted differently.[6]

And again elsewhere Hick says that

> We cannot help 'having' a stream of sense experiences; and we cannot help accepting this as the perception of a material world around us in space. When we open our eyes in daylight we cannot but receive the visual experiences that come to us; and likewise with the other senses.[7]

Hick is suggesting that there is a world of objects around us, but that our consciousness of the world is based upon contact with sense data and not contact with the physical environment itself. While I am not accusing Hick of being a classical sense datum theorist, Hick does seem to be using a version of the theory in which sense data create a layer between the perceiver and the objects perceived. Having assumed in this fashion that we do not have contact with the world, Hick accordingly thinks it is then possible to question the existence of the external world. We will examine the legitimacy and some of the implications of this assumption more carefully later. We will find that Hick's assumption is not necessarily supported by our experience of the world, and that he seems simply to posit this assumption in support of his position. Before indicating this more clearly, however, I want to bring in his understanding of religious experience.

Parallel to his account of ordinary experience of the physical world is Hick's understanding of religious experience which has developed in the previous chapter. Hick thinks that religious experience differs from nonreligious experience only as a way of experiencing the same world. "Events which can be experienced as having a purely natural significance are experienced by the religious mind as having also and at the same time religious significance and as mediating the presence and activity of God."[8] The great exemplars of faith, such as Jesus, Paul, and Anselm, had such an awareness of God that God was as indubitable and vivid a factor in their experience as was their physical environment. "They could no more help believing in the reality of God than in the reality of the material world and of their human neighbours."[9] Hick believes that

> God was known to the prophets and apostles as a dynamic will interacting with their own wills; a sheerly given personal reality, as inescapably to be reckoned with as a destructive storm and life-giving sunshine, the fixed contours of the land, or the hatred of their enemies and the friendship of their neighbours.[10]

Hick thus thinks that questions about the veridicality of religious experience should concern those whose experience of God has the compelling quality of that of the prophets and apostles. Such people are no more inclined to doubt the veridical character of their religious experience than they are to doubt the evidence of their senses. But, Hick asks, is it rational for the religious person to take both of these ways of experiencing his or her total environment as knowledge by which to act? Since the givenness or involuntary character of sense experience along with the fact that people can successfully live in terms of it are also characteristic of the type of religious experience Hick is considering, he thinks the answer is yes.

> The sense of the presence of God reported by the great religious figures has a similar involuntary and compelling quality; and as they proceed to live on the basis of it they are sustained and confirmed by their further experiences in the conviction that they are living in relation, not to illusion, but to reality. It therefore seems *prima facie*, that the religious man is entitled to trust his religious experience and to proceed to conduct his life in terms of it.[11]

In reaching this conclusion, Hick means to be depending upon an analogy between normal acceptance of sense experience as a phenomenal awareness of the objective external world, and a corresponding acceptance of the religious experience of living in the unseen presence of God as the phenomenal awareness of a divine noumenal reality.[12] "In each case there is a solipsist alternative in which one can affirm *solus ipse* to the exclusion of the transcendent—in the one case denying a physical environment transcending our own private consciousness, and in the other case denying a divine Mind transcending our own private consciousness."[13] Hick is emphatic that this analogy is not grounded either in the perception of particular material objects or the contrast between veridical and illusory sense perceptions, but it is grounded in the contrast between a normal awareness of an objective external world and a solipsist interpretation of the same stream of consciousness.

Though Hick is not intending to use a contrast between veridical and illusory sense perceptions, it may be helpful to consider some of the weaknesses of the views of those who have used this contrast. We will look to the work of the late Oxford don, J. L. Austin, in his lecture series that was bound and titled *Sense and Sensibilia*.[14]

Though *Sense and Sensibilia* is packed with various arguments, Austin's overall purpose in this lecture series seems to have been first to demolish the doctrine that we never directly perceive material objects, but only sense data, and then secondly to attack the distinction between incorrigible sense-datum statements and corrigible material object ones. Sense datum statements are those which are thought by some to provide evidence for all others and are such that one cannot be in error in believing or disbelieving them, in contrast to corrigible material object statements which can never be fully verified. Austin's assault on the sense data doctrine will be the focus here, and we shall only deal with the main thrust of his arguments in these areas.

Austin charges that A. J. Ayer and others have skillfully worked the notion that since much of our perception is plagued with illusion, as when a straight stick appears bent while it is partially submerged in water, we must not experience material things in the world as they really are.[15] Without going into the details of any one version of the argument from illusion, as Austin did, we should yet see Austin's contention that this argument is preparing the ground for a huge bogus dichotomy. Instead of having contact with the world, we soon find ourselves concluding that we only perceive sense data. But Austin asks whether this is true.[16]

> What is wrong, what is even faintly surprising, in the idea of a stick's being straight but looking bent sometimes? Does anyone suppose that if something is straight, then it jolly well has to look straight at all times and in all circumstances? Obviously no one seriously supposes this. So what mess are we supposed to get into here, what is the difficulty?[17]

But accepting much of the argument from illusion,

> [Ayer]...sometimes speaks *as if* only sense-data in fact existed, and *as if* "material things" were really just jig-saw constructions of sense-data. It is clear that he is actually taking this to be true. For he holds without question that empirical "evidence" is supplied only by the occurrence of sense-data, and that it is *for this reason* that "any proposition that refers to a material thing *must somehow* be expressible in terms of sense-data, if it is to be empirically significant."[18]

Ayer and the others want us to believe there are two levels, thinks Austin, one of the real world and the other of sense data about the world. Our minds being insulated from the real world by sense data, it turns out to be a mistake to say that we have direct confirmation of events in the world, for we only have indirect means of confirmation through sense data.

Though Hick does not use the argument from illusion, the type of dichotomy that Ayer supports with this argument is important to Hick. For as we have seen, Hick's argument for the rationality of religious belief seems to entail such a dichotomy. Hick thinks that, just as it is rational to believe in the existence of an external world even though we only have a phenomenal awareness of it, likewise it is also rational to believe in a divine noumenal reality on the basis of one's religious experience even though people can only have a phenomenal awareness of God. But if the dichotomy by which people are thought to be limited to a phenomenal awareness of the world is unfounded, Hick's analogy between ordinary and religious experience seems to break down. For if our belief in the external world is simply required by our contact with the world itself (in some critical realist sense), this belief would be quite unlike religious belief, since religious experience, according to Hick, is a supplemental interpretation that is not identified with ordinary objects and events, but is somehow complementary to them. Talk about the world of objects and events would naturally be considered cognitive, then, because of the objective character of the world, while talk about God would not have this cognitive basis. Hick would thus no longer have grounds to argue that if it is rational to believe in an external world, it is also rational to believe in God. Hick must therefore maintain that we only have a phenomenal awareness of the world, not actual contact with it, or he will lose his argument for the rationality of religious belief.

What means Hick might use to maintain this dichotomy are not clear. He is surely aware of the problems with the argument from illusion.[19] In response to Austin's polemic, many thinkers, including Ayer, have suggested that the argument from illusion, when properly stated, supplies only a motive for adopting the sense datum terminology.[20] Hick himself seems merely to assume that people are insulated from the world by sense data, the existence of which are inferred from a description of how we perceive. Hick says that information passes in the form of light waves from a lighted object to the retina of the eye, is there transformed into chemical changes in the rods and cones, and then into electrical impulses passing up the strands of the optic nerve into the brain, and finally into the conscious experience of seeing the object which had been reflecting light into our eyes.[21]

But as mentioned in chapter III, the mind itself is thought to play an important role in organizing the information that reaches us from our environment.

In this procedure—which constitutes normal perception—the function of our system of concepts, or recognitional capacities, is to guide the pre-conscious interpretive process whereby sensory information is transformed into our actual consciousness of the world.[22]

Here Hick has moved from a mechanical description of how we see to a statement about that of which we have consciousness through sensory information. In so doing, he might well have distinguished more sharply between the mechanical description of *how* we see something from consciousness of *what* we see, for a mechanistic physicalist explanation of how we see is markedly different from what we see. We envision or picture reality in conjunction with feelings and values in a way that does not resemble a mechanical description of physical causal interactions. There is continuity and cumulative identity between the one who experiences and the thing experienced. So although a theory of perception may account for one's experience of the world by way of photons and light waves, this account does not necessitate that we see sense data. We believe we see objects. If people are mistaken in thinking that they experience objects directly (in the critical realist sense), Hick should explain why this is. But he has not done so. He simply moves from a mechanical description of how we experience to an assumption that what we experience is not the world, even though this assumption does not necessarily follow. An example in which there is a series of causal interactions similar to those in Hick's description of perception may illustrate this issue.

One could use an oscilloscope to monitor the electrical output of a diesel generator.[23] Were the generator in a fairly sophisticated setting such as is found in an ocean-going ship or a scientific station in Antarctica, one could plug into the electrical current directly at the generator, or one could plug into the line some distance from the generator after the output had been transformed to a higher voltage, or one could plug into the line at a place where the output had been changed from alternating current to direct current at a low voltage. In each instance, one would be correct in saying that the electrical output of the generator had been monitored, if in fact this is what was done, even though there was a chain of intermediate events between the generator and the place in the line at which the output was monitored. At one place the generator's output was seen through alternative current, at another through high voltage, and at another through low voltage direct current. Similarly, it may be that the visual sensation of some object involves a series of causal interactions including light waves traveling from the object that are focused by the lens of the eye upon the retina, and so forth, and that any segment of this process might correctly be evaluated as an affect of the object from which the light traveled, despite the nature of this segment of the chain of interactions through which the transmission of this affect occurred.

In the same way, critical realists try to recognize physical things as the objects of sensory experience. Perceiving is thought to be a complex operation through which sensory appearances are characterized by judgment and belief (up to this point Hick would agree), but the critical realist departs from Hick by understanding perception as direct awareness of or confrontation with external objects. The critical realist is attempting to do justice in an empirical manner not only to the analysis of perception in terms of sensory data but also to the unshakeable belief in observed things.[24] Hick, however, sometimes so emphasizes sense data as the only distinct objects of perception that he also feels comfortable in further entertaining the solipsist possibility that there is no world independent of one's sense experiences. As was quoted earlier, Hick says that although solipsism is a possible interpretation of our sense experience, this "...does not indicate that our normal interpretation of our sense experience is doubtful, but that despite its indubitable character it is nevertheless an interpretation of data which are capable of being interpreted differently."[25] Were it not for his willingness to entertain this solipsist possibility, Hick otherwise would sound as though he were a critical realist. At one place Hick says, "...the world which we...perceive is not plastic to our wishes but presents itself to us as it is, whether we like it or not."[26] Or again, Hick says most adamantly that if one could reject that one's consciousness is reliably affected by the surrounding physical world, "...it would amount to an act of intellectual suicide."[27]

The adequacy of critical realism or any other theory of perception should not concern us,[28] except as Hick construes it in his attempt to show the rationality of religious belief. What is required for my argument is that we see that Hick does not have a good analogy between ordinary and religious experience. He tells us that just as there may be a world that transcends our sense experience, there may also be a God that transcends our religious experience. But one of the problems with this analogy is that Hick sets us up for it with his account of ordinary experience. He tells us we are at least within our rights to believe there is an external world that transcends our phenomenal awareness of it, as though we might not believe this. Hick has thus made ordinary experience of the world appear to be like experience of the transcendent God. But to the contrary, as we have seen all along, he actually believes on the one hand that it would amount to intellectual suicide to doubt the indubitable character of the material environment, and on the other hand, that it is always possible for one to doubt the veracity of one's religious experience. If the present world's circumstances did not in Hick's view always allow people to doubt the truth of claims about the presence and purpose of God, Hick would not have promoted his notion of eschatological verification.

Hick may think there is no inconsistency in talking as though the physical environment transcends one's awareness of it and yet that people at the same time cannot sanely doubt its existence. As we have seen, the reason he may think there is no inconsistency is both because of his stress upon interpretation in perception and because of the supposed gap between the perceiver and the object perceived. The weakness in Hick's thinking about perception with which I have been concerned here, however, is that he seems to manage to insulate the perceiver from the world by merely assuming the truth of a particular version of sense datum theory. In that he maintains that this version of sense datum theory is correct, it seems that he is committing intellectual suicide, as he refers to it, since it is by means of his concept of sense data that he entertains the possibility that a person's consciousness of the world (as the solipsist would have it) is not affected by an external physical environment.

It does not matter that Hick is in good company with Ayer in making this assumption involving sense data. Hick should provide justification for his view of sense datum theory, or else he should come up with some other means of showing that people do not actually have contact with the world. If Hick cannot show this, he seems to lose his analogy between ordinary and religious experience, and hence also his argument for the rationality of religious belief. For ordinary experience of the material environment seems to be quite different from religious experience. The former is objective in character while the latter in contrast is more subjective. Considering some of these differences will further illustrate the dissimilarity between ordinary experience and Hick's concept of experience of God.

2. Ordinary and Religious Experience

One of the most obvious differences between ordinary and religious experience has to do with the fact that while we cannot keep from having experiences of the world, we are not obliged to interact consciously with a spiritual environment. Ordinary experience is coercive. The world exerts control over our experience of it, but religious experience is thought in contrast to be the result of an uncompelled response of faith. In one of the examples we have seen in several earlier chapters here, for instance, the Chaldeans were making war upon Jerusalem, and according to Hick, the prophet Jeremiah experienced this event as the judgment of God upon Israel. Those involved in the actual battle, however, must have experienced the events naturalistically, if they were to survive, and they may have had no religious faith regarding these events whatsoever. What is essential to the soldier is the compelling quality of ordinary experience. Presumably (from the naturalist's viewpoint) those soldiers who were alert to the enemy archers would have been a lot better off than someone so absorbed in a religious experience that he might not have been aware of the enemy arrows.

Being shot by an arrow and other such possibilities provide grounds or public criteria by which to decide whether or not ordinary experience (such as fighting a group of Chaldeans) is veridical, but there are no such criteria, that I can detect, by which to check the veracity of religious experience as Hick understands it. For the religious experience is in Hick's way of thinking an interpretation that complements ordinary levels of experience so as to allow the religious aspect to be ignored if a person so chooses. And if one chooses not to experience the world religiously, it seems that his or her ability to live life is only affected with regard to the type of moral policies and patterns of behavior that he or she may adopt. Hick believes the fully God-conscious person should "...see self and neighbour as objects of the same divine love, and as called to mutual service each as God's agent in relation to the other."[29] But it is not clear that being motivated to emulate Jesus' life style in any way provides grounds for determining the veracity of an experience of God. The egotistical naturalist may feel that Pontius Pilate lived a much better life style than Jesus did.

As we have seen, Hick attempts to cope with the compelling quality of ordinary experience in contrast to the tacit presence of one's supplemental religious awareness by arguing that prior to one's coming to be aware of God, one is cognitively free in relation to God. "And yet once a man has allowed himself freely to become conscious of God—it is important to note—that experience is, at its top levels of intensity, coercive."[30] The apostle, prophet, or saint can be so vividly aware of God that he or she can no more doubt the veracity of his or her awareness of God than he or she can doubt his or her sense perception.

But few people have as vivid and coercive a religious experience as that reported by the great biblical figures. So the majority of us may be entitled to wonder whether religious experience is delusive, perhaps somewhat like that of the paranoiac who hears threatening voices from the radiator or the drug addict who sees a pink aura around some object upon which he or she may focus. That people can act in accord with some supplemental delusive experiences makes them no less delusive.

Normal people might think that since religious experience is an interpretation of significance that in Hick's view only supplements ordinary coercive experience of objects and events of the world, the religious experience might very well be delusive. It can be explained in terms of abnormal psychology as a product of disorientation, unproductive pathology, buried infantile memory, and the like. Religious experience would thus be considered nonveridical and religious beliefs irrational in contrast to ordinary experience of and belief in the material environment.

Those who think religious language is noncognitive might further argue that the many different religious traditions of the world help make their case. People tend to adopt the religion of the region in which they are raised. One born in India would probably be a Hindu, one born in Egypt would perhaps be a Muslim, in Ceylon a Buddhist, or in America a Christian. But each of these different religions professes to be true. Should we therefore expect that one is true while the others false, perhaps wondering whether they are equally false or possibly only false in varying degrees? Or might we expect that each is subjectively true for its own adherents while in fact none is true objectively?[31]

Further eroding Hick's analogy between experience of the material world and religious experience is the immense variety and number of forms of religious experience. The Christian, Buddhist, Hindu, and Moslem each seems to have a different form of religious experience and belief. In contrast to this, ordinary human experience reveals a world which is public in that normally the awareness of several individuals can be correlated in terms of a common world which they jointly inhabit.[32]

Hick replies that the different religious experiences may also be correlated in terms of a single divine reality. As noted earlier, Hick argues that the "...divine reality has always been self-revealingly active towards mankind, and that the differences of human response are related to different human circumstances."[33] The ethnic, geographical, climatic, economic, sociological, and historical circumstances have produced the various existing human cultures, and within each main cultural region a response to the divine has taken its own form. The "...resulting large-scale religio-cultural phenomena are what we call the religions of the world."[34] Hick is "...suggesting that God is to be thought of as the divine noumenon, experienced by mankind as a range of divine phenomena which take both theistic and non-theistic forms."[35] Functioning in a role analogous to that of time in the schematization of the Kantian categories

> ...is the continuum of historical factors which have produced our different religious cultures. It is the variations of the human cultural situation that concretize the notion of deity as specific images of God. And it is these images that inform man's actual religious experience, so that it is an experience specifically of the God of Israel, or of Allah, or of the Father of our Lord Jesus Christ, or of Vishnu or Shiva.[36]

But given this distinction between phenomena and divine noumena, Hick recognizes that some people will think it should be impossible to have an account of the divine nature. "For if we only know God as experienced by mankind, and if God is so experienced in a number of different ways, does not the noumenal or real God remain impenetrably hidden from us?"[37] The answer, according to Hick, is no. He thinks that if we can accept that the infinite divine reality somehow impinges upon finite human consciousness, "...then the very plurality and variety of human experiences of God provides a wider basis for theology than can the experience of any one religious tradition taken by itself."[38] Hick further believes, as we have seen, that unless we have the ability to shut God out of our consciousness, we would lose our freedom over against the infinite divine reality. As absolute value supposedly makes a claim upon us, we preserve our freedom by being aware of the absolute in terms of limited concepts and images.

This attempt to correlate the various religious experiences and beliefs will nevertheless not eliminate some of the crucial differences between ordinary and religious types of experiences. For example again, although people might ordinarily see a distant object as a rabbit or a stump of a tree or as a tuft of grass, there are public criteria by which a person can find out which it actually is. If the object moves, the observers can be pretty sure it is not a tree stump. And if the observers are hunters, they might shoot the object and then examine it closely. Were the object a rabbit, they would find a soft, furry creature with blood on it, and so forth. But it does not seem that in Hick's way of thinking there are such criteria by which to identify God; for God is outside ordinary experience except as an interpreted religious significance that is thought to supplement ordinary experience of the material environment. The description of this awareness or significance may range from that of a nonpersonal void (perhaps in the Buddhist tradition) to a personal immanent Being (in the Western tradition), and there does not seem to be any criteria of the sort we find with ordinary experience by which to grade these many diverse types of religious experience.

3. The Result

Religious awareness is thus dissimilar to ordinary experience because it does not seem to have the same empirical basis. Objects and events exert some control over ordinary experience, while God seems to impress people in nearly any way imaginable, even sometimes in ways that seem to exclude the other possibilities, as when God is conceived to be nothingness. So while Hick is free to postulate a divine noumenal reality that supposedly lies behind the various conceptions of God, the only way Hick could justify doing this would be by showing that it is rational to consider each type of religious experience veridical, which we have seen he has not done. His argument for the rationality of religious experience depends upon an analogy between ordinary and religious experience that does not hold once his use of sense datum theory is called into question. It does not seem that we are so insulated from the world by sense data that we can legitimately discount the existence of the world, though many people do seem honestly to doubt the existence of God. Hick accordingly seems to be without means to show that religious experience is rational.

More importantly, given the lack of empirical basis for theistic experience, on Hick's account, such experience may be purely subjective, in which case talk about a divine noumenal reality would by Hick's own reckoning be noncognitive and oftentimes meaningless. As we have seen in chapters I through III, religious utterances are thought to be noncognitive if they do not have to do with an objective state of affairs that can be experienced independently of one's mental state.

If religious experience seems to be irrational and unrelated to ordinary experience, a consequence of this is that we should doubt that assertions based upon it are true. All sorts of crazy things are predicted and we pay no attention to them. People talk about the eventual dawning of pyramid power or the earth being taken over by Martians, and we think they are spouting nonsense because we know of no evidences for these claims. Although they can be considered factual or cognitive in a mere technical sense, again according to the criteria developed in chapters I through III (they predict what could in-principle be verified), such assertions are nevertheless thought to be false. Would it be prudent to think that a Mariner space probe will one day return to the earth filled with cream cheese? Obviously not, in spite of the fact that someone could predict such an event. And the notion of an eschatological situation in which people are conscious of the unseen presence and purpose of God is similarly absurd unless there is a plausible basis for it. But Hick's account of religious experience, as we have seen, only provides a questionable basis for his eschatological predictions.

Unless Hick can show that religious experience is veridical, it seems that he has no cause to suggest an eschatological situation. Hick has himself used this line of reasoning against the medieval principal of plenitude. This is the principle that, for the universe to be as perfect as is possible, it must contain as many diverse kinds of objects as possible. This principle explained the distinctions and inequalities among the varieties of possible kinds of creatures as the product of the creative capacity of God. In order for this principle to be an adequate explanation, Hick says there is required the speculation that the universe is infinite in an infinite number of ways and that somewhere in it are realized all the possible forms of life, including an array of centaurs, griffins, mermaids, and unicorns. Hick, however, rejects this speculation because he thinks it is entirely unrelated to human experience. He says that to affirm that there are mermaids and centaurs somewhere in the universe, in that it is a conceptual possibility that there are, is to have turned from rational speculation into uncontrolled fantasy.[39] Hick likewise (were he to impose his requirements upon himself) seems to be in no position to promote the notion of eschatological verification. For although it is logically possible to predict an eschatological situation, there is hardly more evidence for an eschaton, in Hick's way of thinking, than there is for other worlds full of centaurs and unicorns. How can he on the one hand be assured of an eschaton and on the other hand reject the implications of the principle of plenitude? After all, there are people who are just as inclined to believe in the existence of such creatures as some theists are inclined to believe in an eschaton.[40]

The notion of an eschatological situation in which verification of theistic assertions would occur is seemingly little more plausible than another world where there are unicorns, for Hick has not established the rationality of the religious beliefs upon which eschatological predictions are based. Some of the implications of this conclusion will be brought together in the next chapter.

NOTES

[1]John Hick, *Faith and Knowledge* (2nd ed.; Cleveland: Fount Paperbacks, 1978), p. 109.

[2]Ibid.

[3]Ibid., p. 110.

[4]John Hick, *Arguments for the Existence of God* (New York: The Seabury Press, 1971), p. 110.

[5]Hick, *Faith and Knowledge*, p. 110.

[6]John Hick, *The Center of Christianity* (New York: Harper and Row, Publishers, 1978), pp. 46-47.

[7]Hick, *Arguments for the Existence of God*, p. 113.

[8]Ibid., p. 111.

[9]Ibid., p. 112.

[10]Ibid.

[11]Ibid.

[12]Ibid. Although Hick does not use the terms "phenomenal" and "noumenal" in discussing his analogy between ordinary and religious types of experience, that he could use these terms in discussing this supposed analogy is implied by his work cited in notes 1 through 3 above and note 12 of chapter I.

[13]Ibid., p. 113.

[14]J. L. Austin, *Sense and Sensibilia* (Oxford: Oxford University Press, 1962).

[15]Ibid., pp. 61-63. According to A. J. Ayer, in his *The Foundations of Empirical Knowledge* (New York: St. Martin's Press, 1963), ch. 1, the argument from illusion is as follows. Material things may present different appearances to different observers in different situations, or even to the same observer in different conditions. A material thing cannot have all of the properties it seems to observers to have. Therefore, when observers perceive a material thing as having properties other than it has, they cannot be perceiving a material thing but rather a sense datum. Ayer then has several arguments by which he intends to show that we always perceive sense data. First, an observer sometimes cannot distinguish a veridical perception from a delusory perception (i.e., there is no intrinsic difference in kind). If veridical perception were of material things, and delusory perception of sense data, we would expect these experiences to be different, but they are not. So, we always experience sense data in perception. Second, veridical and delusory perceptions form a continuous series with respect to their qualities and to the conditions in which they are obtained. Veridical and delusory perceptions are generically the same. Hence again, we always experience sense data in perception. Third, one's object of immediate awareness depends on external factors. Material objects and their properties are not dependent on external factors. Thus, material objects are not the objects of immediate awareness. (I am indebted to Ann Garry

of California State University at Los Angeles for this summary of Ayer's arguments).

[16]Austin, *Sense and Sensibilia*, p. 47.

[17]Ibid., p. 29.

[18]Ibid., p. 107.

[19]According to Austin, some of the problems with the argument from illusion are as follows. (a) Perception does not fall into two groups, the "delusive" and the "veridical," and this mistake trades upon not distinguishing illusions from delusions (Ibid., p. 54) The term "illusion" does not mean that something unreal is conjured up in contradistinction to the term "delusion." When one has a delusion, he may be in serious trouble. Yet when I see an optical illusion, there is nothing personally wrong with me, says Austin; it is something quite public that anyone can see. But the argument from illusion tends first to parade cases of illusion with the implication that there really is something there, then quietly calls these cases delusive and therefore slips in the idea that the thing perceived is an immaterial sense datum (Ibid., p. 25). (b) There is an implicit but grotesque exaggeration of the frequency of delusive perceptions (c) and another exaggeration of the similarity between delusive and veridical perceptions. That people fail to distinguish between hallucinations and genuine perceptions does not mean that they are not distinguishable; (d) and even if on rare occasions they are indistinguishable and thus perhaps delusions are thought to be sense data (though there is no reason to think so), this would still not warrant the extension of sense data to the normal cases of perception (Ibid., p. 52).

[20]A. J. Ayer, "Rejoinder to Professor Ferguson," in *Symposium on J. L. Austin*, ed. by K. T. Fann (New York: Humanities Press, 1969), pp. 346, 354.

[21]John Hick, "Towards a Philosophy of Religious Pluralism," *Neue Zeitschrift fur systematische Theologie*, Vol. 22, No. 2 (1980), p. 139.

[22]Ibid., p. 140.

[23]I used this method myself at Byrd VLF Station (Longwire) in Antarctica. There were several places in the station (Stanford's lab, University of Washington's lab, and sometimes the generator room) where there were oscilloscopes that could be used to check the quality of the output from the generators.

[24]See for example A. 0. Lovejoy, "The Justification of Realism," and R. W. Sellars, "The Aim of Critical Realism," in *Perception and the External World*, ed. by R. J. Hirst (New York: The Macmillan Company, 1965), pp. 224-244.

[25]Hick, *The Center of Christianity*, pp. 46-47.

[26]Hick, *Arguments for the Existence of God*, p. 113.

[27]Hick, *The Center of Christianity*, p. 52.

[28]For critical interaction with the various theories of perception, see R. J. Hirst, ed., *Perception and the External World*, and D. J. O'Connor and Brian Carr, *Introduction to the Theory of Knowledge* (Minneapolis: University of Minnesota Press, 1982), ch. IV.

[29]John Hick, *The Center of Christianity* (New York: Harper and Row, Publishers, 1978), p. 64.

[30]Hick, *Arguments for the Existence of God*, p. 114.

[31]John Hick, *God and the Universe of Faiths* (London: The Macmillan Press, 1973), p. 100. Hick here entertains the question at hand. His reply to this question can be seen in the material cited in notes 33 through 38 below.

[32]Hick makes this observation himself in *Arguments for the Existence of God*, p. 117. His attempt to cope with this situation can again be seen in the material cited in notes 33 through 38 below.

[33]Hick, *God and the Universe of Faiths*, p. 138.

[34]Ibid., p. 143.

[35]Hick, "Towards a Philosophy of Religious Pluralism," p. 146.

[36]Ibid., p. 143.

[37]Ibid., p. 146.

[38]Ibid.

[39]John Hick, *Evil and the God of Love* (San Francisco: Harper and Row, Publishers, 1978), pp. 70-82.

[40]See for example Rien Poortuliet and Wil Huygen, *Gnomes* (New York: Bantam Books, 1979), and Rudiger Robert Beer, *The Unicorn: Myth and Reality* (New York: Van Nos Reinhold, 1977).

CHAPTER VI

CONCLUSION

The foregoing indicates that Hick has not yet recognized an obstacle that may block his effort to create a global theology. Certain methodological factors in his system of thought that do lend themselves to such a theology tend to hide this problem. Among these factors is that his theological concern allows him to propose a theory by which the plurality of world religions might be pulled together into a universal scheme. That is, he does not see any one religion as necessarily superior to the others. Hick's neo-analytic methodology most likely even allows him to state his pluralist theory in a technical sense as a matter of fact. For given the viability of his methodology, he may be able to predict an eschatological situation in which his theory could in principle be verified, this verifiability in turn giving this theory its cognitive status.[1]

But the cardinal problem that Hick apparently does not see is that his eschatological prediction does not seem to have empirical warrant. The existence of the different world religions and their ways of accounting for God are not in themselves sufficient grounds for his pluralist hypothesis. To the contrary, their existence suggests that the imagined relationship between these religious phenomena and a common divine reality is incredible. There is often conflict between the major religions at nearly every level. An examination of most scholarly studies in comparative religion will demonstrate the extent of the disparity between them, but for the purpose of the present study, it may be best to consider a recent statement from Hick. He says of himself:

In the article 'On Grading Religions' I made a number of suggestions for criteria by which to assess particular religious phenomena—the founding figures, systems of doctrine, mythologies, social and historical outworkings—and I shall not repeat these here. I concluded that 'whilst we can to some extent assess and grade religious phenomena, we cannot realistically assess and grade the great world religions as totalities. For each of these long traditions is so internally diverse, containing so many kinds of both good and evil, that it is impossible for human judgment to weigh them up and compare their merits as systems of salvation. It may be that one facilitates human liberation/salvation more than the others; but if so this is not evident to human vision' (p. 467).[2]

What Hick has said here raises the question at issue. He is sensitive to some of the factors that make it difficult for him to unite the plurality of religions in that he admits that these religions cannot be assessed either as totalities or with regard to their soteriological adequacy. In the next paragraph he nevertheless continues to contend

...that the differences of belief between (and within) the traditions are legion, but that it is important to distinguish their various levels. These include differences of historical fact, which are in principle settleable now though in practice often not; differences of what might be called metaphysical fact (e.g. reincarnation), which are settleable eschatologically but probably not now; and differences of mythology and doctrinal interpretation, constituting systems which may well be analogous to alternative maps, in different projections, of the universe. These different differences both arise from and help to constitute different perceptions of the divine from within different forms of human life.[3]

Here Hick has reverted to his standard line. Acknowledging the tremendous differences between the religious traditions, he yet assumes that they all relate to the same ultimate divine reality. That he is making this assumption is clear from the following statement made earlier in the same article. "And by pluralism," he says, "I mean the view—which I advocate— that the great world faiths embody different perceptions and conceptions of...the Real or the Ultimate."[4]

That Hick advocates this pluralism as fact, I am suggesting, is at variance with the larger part of his system of thought. As we have seen in his handling of the medieval principle of plenitude at the end of the previous chapter, and as anyone who is familiar with his work knows, Hick does not usually hesitate to impose the evidentualist requirements of his system upon others with whom he disagrees. For example, against those types of theodicy that incorporate Satan and the satanic kingdom, Hick says that the discussion of the problem of evil in these cases is thrown "...into metaphysical regions in relation to which the already sufficient difficulties of knowing whether we are talking sense or nonsense are compounded to a point that is, literally, beyond all reason."[5] Granting Hick's contention, it is puzzling that on the one hand he dismisses talk of a satanic being in dealing with the problem of evil, while on the other hand he tries to hang on to quite disparate world religions when he speaks of God. This religious pluralism might be commendable were he only intending to promote a more stable world community, but if so, he has misled his readers. He implies that his theology is a matter of fact, even though he has not shown that its metaphysical regions are any less ethereal than those involving Satan. Hick's problem is that in order to have sufficient factual basis for his theological discussion, he needs more than an other-worldly eschatological hypothesis; he needs some this-worldly evidence by which to correlate the world's diverse religions. In doggedly assuming the feasibility of his global theology despite his lack of evidence for it, he has failed to impose his own evidentualist standards upon himself. He simply gives himself a privileged position.

That Hick's global theology is then mostly an *ad hoc* creation does not necessarily affect other well-known figures in this field, two of whom I should mention in passing. Ninian Smart and Wilfred Cantwell Smith are both highly respected for their attempts to develop a world theology.[6] Smart's thesis, which he refers to as transcendental pluralism, is much like Hick's view in that it postulates a single divine reality beyond the different experiences of it. Though Smart is more tentative than Hick in advancing this theory, he is criticized, as is Hick, for misrepresenting the different religious traditions in order to synthesize them.[7] Smith on the other hand openly admits that a successful synthesis of the conflicting truth claims of the world religions is interlinked with the as yet uncompleted task of attaining epistemological sophistication.[8] Smith seems to believe, as Hick does not, that a static empiricist approach to the different religions will not resolve their conflicting claims. This particular belief of Smith is supported by the present study.

Perhaps a bit less evident, but no less important, are several other implications of the present study that I will now try to draw out in two respects: the first with regard to what remains of Hick's system after my criticisms have been taken into account, and the second with regard to how related studies in philosophy of religion might best proceed.

Finding as we have that eschatological verification is not a vital component of Hick's system of thought is significant because it upsets his distinction between naturalism and theism. As I have set forth the issue in the second section of the first chapter, Hick's position leaves both the naturalist and the theist in their respective territories to do whatever it is they do. The situation might be caricatured as though the naturalist is able to carry on with science without being bothered by the religious person's contemplation of God. Eschatological verification attempts to legitimate talk about God, but in doing so, it incorporates the basic naturalist contention that there is currently no objective evidence provided by the material environment by which to verify theistic claims. The religious experience through which verification might occur, were it not for the problem of evil, is described as a psychological perspective which only supplements the perception of ordinary objects and events. This psychological aspect of religious experience does not necessarily give it a lesser metaphysical status, in Hick's way of thinking, because ordinary experience of the world is on the other hand also thought to be a matter of interpretation or experiencing-as. But religious experience always remains suspect as a result of the problem of evil or suffering in the world. My argument in the last section of chapter IV attempted to turn this around by showing that the experience of evil does not in principle set up the problem in Hick's system that he claims it does, so that eschatological verification is found not to be essential to his thinking. This conclusion paves the way for the encroachment of theism upon naturalism. For if the existence of evil is not an intractable problem for the theist, the naturalist and the theist are left on more equal footing. The theist does not need to speculate about a future eschatological situation in that the experiential conditions which Hick requires of verification can be obtained here and now. In the course of seeing this, however, we also found that the notion of an eschatological situation is vitally dependent, as is all of Hick's religious thought, upon his conception of religious experience.

Questioning the veracity of religious experience cuts deeply into Hick's entire conceptual edifice and seems to endanger the lesser of its two basic parts. It appears that the religious part is only subjectively imposed upon the more basic part made up of naturalism. Underneath the layer of world religions that Hick is attempting to correlate with his global theology is his account of naturalism, which seems to be left in place once the religious part is separated off.

It thus seems that Hick has created a theology that favors the naturalist. Hick's religious views are not intended to conflict with the naturalist suppositions of the sciences, as long as these suppositions are not atheistic, but rather seem to be checked by the sciences. Hick believes that prescientific religious traditions, such as that Jesus Christ was God incarnate or any other similar poetic mythological concept, should be left behind as they are seen to conflict with the discoveries of science.[9] But the solid core of naturalism, as Hick describes it, remains foundational.

This does not mean that Hick's naturalist suppositions are true. In the first section of chapter IV, we saw that Hick has not shown that the world is religiously ambiguous, and it is conceivable that the universe may provide evidence in favor of theism. As unlikely as this is usually thought to be, and though an examination of evidentualist theistic claims is far beyond the scope of this study, I will at least touch upon that which may constitute theistic evidence for some thinkers in the latter part of this chapter.

There are obviously other types of criticism of Hick's thinking that I have left aside. As I stipulated in the first chapter, Hick's understanding of the various issues of philosophy of language and religion, involving confirmation theory, have been assumed to be adequate for the evaluation of religious claims.[10] But his views may not be adequate. There are those who argue that no account of confirmation is acceptable, because they think there is no way to determine what should constitute confirmation for any one individual with regard to any one set of circumstances,[11] and then there are those who support confirmation theory because they think its problems are not insurmountable.[12] Complicating the issues between these two groups are those thinkers we saw in chapter II, represented by W. T. Jones, who simply make the crude assumption that there is no God by which to confirm theistic talk, as well as those like Alvin Plantinga who think that, were a theory of confirmation as a criterion of meaning adequate, it must include the possibility of confirmation of theism.[13] But to have gone off into these various issues involving philosophy of language would have detracted from the examination of the views of Hick.

That Hick's system seems to reduce to its naturalist part is quite a serious problem. Talk about God in many instances becomes a noncognitive expression of the thoughts and actions of those who simply have a religious way of life. Unless God is truly an ontological reality, as religious people usually think is the case, Hick believes that he and others would give up the theistic tradition. There are of course ways in which Hick and other theists like him might cope with this problem. In the remarks that follow, we will look at some of the implications of the present study for one of the ways in which this might be done. The views of W. T. Jones that we examined in chapter II will be useful for this purpose.

According to Jones, we can recall, our perceptual field includes as foreground whatever is immediately experienced, and as background what we hope and believe to be true of our immediate experience of the world. Our perceptual field at any one moment is thought to be the product of mutual interaction between foreground and background. As an example of this, Jones suggests that when Galileo looked into the night sky on January 7, 1610, he saw three fixed stars; the Ptolemaic scheme in his background structure dictated that every bright spot in the night sky, besides those believed to be the seven planets, were stars.[14] But sometime shortly thereafter, Galileo's foreground changed, for instead of stars he saw the moons of Jupiter, which new insight apparently arose from a new background structure provided by the Copernican model of the universe. This type of change similarly occurred when thinkers adopted the evolutionary account of human origins over against the creationist account. And the same type of change may have been made when scientists replaced Newton's views with the theory of relativity.

The relevance of Jones' approach for Hick is that it illustrates the effect of naturalism in Hick's system. As Jones' analysis would have it, naturalism appears to be a predominant factor in the background structure of Hick's position. Hick's concept of eschatological verification was generated by this segment of his thinking, in that eschatological verification is in part an attempt to overcome the positivist supposition that talk about God is not meaningful. But if Hick could utilize a more comprehensive background structure that is not antithetical to theism, it would perhaps be easier for him to put together a system of thought that would include the religious dimension of human experience. I will try to illustrate this point with the work of George Mavrodes and Saint Anselm.

Mavrodes has attempted to describe experience of God in terms of input-alignment, as he refers to it.[15] In developing this notion, I will not bother to consider how the views of Mavrodes and Hick happen to diverge or mesh, nor will I criticize Mavrodes, but I will go into enough detail to show the basic factor that I believe makes Mavrodes' position superior. After that I will use Anselm in a similar way.

Beginning with a popular view of perception, Mavrodes entertains the notion that an object is a proper visual stimulus only when it transmits light that stimulates the eye directly, the light in no way reflected after being transmitted and affecting one's eyes.[16] Though there can be both generators and reflectors of light, such as the sun and the moon, either of which can transmit light, it depends upon the object as to whether it was a generator or reflector that last transmitted the light directly to the eyes. Mavrodes points out that a consequence of this account is, however, that anyone using a mirror image (an astronomer looking through a telescope to see a planet, a dentist inspecting a tooth through a mirror, a railroad dispatcher watching trains through a television camera) will not be seeing the object he or she aims to be looking at, but only some sort of image. Intermediates such as mirrors, telephones, and television cameras are troublesome for this account because there are occasions when one wants to say one is experiencing the original generating object in spite of the role of the intermediary in retransmitting the light or sound that is perceived. For example, if one heard the echo of someone's voice from the wall of a canyon, one would not be hearing the person speaking but only the cliff (final transmitter) from which the person's voice is echoing. A better account of perception, according to Mavrodes, would somehow bring in the capacity of the one perceiving to constitute the transmitted input in terms of the original source, whether from generator or reflector. But a necessary complication is that people will sometimes be able to experience an object involved in two different sources of input (both generators and reflectors), when on such occasion these people will yet not be able to distinguish between them, as when one looks at the moon through a telescope. In this case one cannot tell the difference between the actual object and the reflection of this object in the mirrors of the telescope, and thus it might be said that these two sources of input are in input-alignment.[17]

When experience involves input-alignment, it seems then to be a matter of judgment on the part of the one perceiving that determines whether it is the generator or the reflector of an object, or both, that is being apprehended. And it seems to follow that if there has been no judgment, then there has been no experience. Mavrodes believes that if this does follow, then experiencing something must have a subjective cognitive aspect that requires a judgment.[18] While light may hit the eye (the microscopist's open eye that is not looking into the instrument), if there is no cognitive activity, then there is no experience. Failing to make a judgment would accordingly be a matter of ignorance, while a false judgment would amount to error. Judgment about an experience of actual objects that is not purely psychological should be correct and the experience a true one if the object to which it refers actually exists, and conversely incorrect and false if the experience is purely psychological.

So Mavrodes thinks that the sense of having an immediate experience of something, though not purely psychological, must have an important psychological aspect. Even though there always seems to be a causal chain of events giving rise to experience (light reflected from an object to the retina of the eye, and so on), the notion of direct experience of an object seems yet to presuppose that there is no intermediate causal chain. Mavrodes thus believes that the feeling or consciousness of directly experiencing an object must be psychological. For the directness of the experience of an object does not consist in the absence of a causal chain.[19] A railroad dispatcher sitting in his or her office, for example, might be keeping tabs on the train yard by means of a television picture. Without reference to the television, this person's thought and judgment could be immediately or directly concerned with the train. So Mavrodes thinks it is possible for people to experience an object and make inferences about it as though they were experiencing it directly, even though they do not have contact with anything other than what mediates the experiencing of it.

Similarly, according to Mavrodes, some people claim to experience God in relation to mundane objects.[20] While they are observing nature or reading Scripture, the experience of God may supervene upon this ordinary physical experience. If it happens to be true that God is the source of all experience, both in terms of past causation and current sustaining activity, then the notion of input-alignment might be used to explain the way in which God supervenes upon ordinary experience. If the world were in total input-alignment with God, it would be possible for people who were experiencing the world to focus their thought and judgment upon God. It could be said therefore that people experience God, and that whenever anyone is experiencing something, one might be experiencing God, though it could not be said that any experience was an experience of God. For as has already been seen in other cases of input-alignment, one might not make the required judgment. We saw that even though one looking in a mirror or at a television set might be making the requisite judgment for the direct experience of the object being mediated, one might also not make the requisite judgment and thus would fail to have the experience.

If this account of religious experience could be maintained, it has an advantage over Hick's account. For Hick believes, as we have seen, that an experience of God is supplemental to ordinary experience of the material environment. In Hick's view, God is a noumenal reality outside of ordinary experience. It is accordingly possible to question the veracity of Hick's view of religious experience. His view seems to have no empirical basis and therefore may be purely subjective, while his account of naturalism on the other hand is left in place. According to Mavrodes' account, however, God is thought to be encountered *in* ordinary experience of the material environment. Any experience could be an experience of God. The background structure of Mavrodes' position does not work against this possibility, and when one is not predisposed against this possibility, the question of what might constitute evidence for theism is put in a new light.

Now one's belief about the nature and acquisition of knowledge would not exclude the possibility of experience of God, which experience, as in the case of the writers of Scripture, could provide substantive realization of such matters as that God continually sustains or maintains and directs the course of the universe. Individuals who have this sort of awareness of God might readily appreciate the classical arguments for the existence of God. Causal, teleological, and moral arguments might carry a great deal of weight for these people because of their predisposition to judge that there is a God fulfilling the requirements suggested by these types of arguments. Saint Anselm's version of the ontological argument is a useful example in this regard.

Saint Anselm of Canterbury is one whose background structure, like that of Mavrodes, can be understood to allow for evidence of God.[21] Central to this interpretation of Anselm is that he believed that reality or derived being is an emanation from the mind of God in which the ideal form of reality exists absolutely. Supposing this is true, since the rational nature of the divine influence upholds human thought processes, Anselm need only offer the notion that that than which nothing greater can be conceived cannot be thought not to exist, and God will cause the logical necessity people realize in analyzing this idea; people are in this way supposedly able to experience God.

In the sixth chapter of the *Proslogium*, Anselm asks how God is sensible, and then reasons that since sensation is for the sake of cognition, one "...who feels obtains knowledge in accordance with the proper functions..."[22] of his or her senses, God also being a possible object of sensation. Even though God does not have a body, Anselm yet thought that God is sensible as the ground of cognition itself. Anselm believed that "...although the truth which is in the existence of things is the effect of the Supreme Truth, this same truth is the cause of the truth which is in a thought and which is in a proposition."[23] God, according to Anselm, is "...that light from which shines every truth that gives light to the rational mind."[24] So if an individual is able to conceive of the necessity of that than which nothing greater can be conceived, Anselm thought this individual would be foolish to turn around and say that such a being is merely a conception of the human mind; for if so, this individual would be caught in the predicament of saying that the magnificent being so apprehended was not in fact the greatest object that can be conceived. Anselm believed that an object that has existence both in the mind and in reality is greater than one which is only an object of conception.

Contemporary criticisms of Anselm's argument typically ignore the background structure upon which it depends. The weight of such criticism is in part the result of placing Anselm's argument in a context in which experience of a transcendent God is thought not to be possible.[25] Hick seems to meander between this naturalist context and the one represented by Anselm, but always by way of a background structure that gives dominance to the suppositions of the naturalist. We have seen the consequence of his doing this, his position apparently reducing to naturalism, whereas other approaches such as those of Mavrodes and Anselm may not include this consequence. In that these other approaches at least give equal force or even dominance to theism, they might be found to be better accounts of the total range of human experience.

Were further study to show that other such approaches are possible and preferable, which I believe is the case, questions about infinite divine attributes, the plurality of world religions, the problem of evil, and the like might each be handled accordingly. But the present study must leave these issues where they lie. Hick's work in these areas has been touched upon, and in some instances it may be quite helpful. It often helpfully explores issues in the history of philosophy and theology, and to this extent it may sometimes serve as a valuable commentary on the various options.

As Hick's methodology has to do with eschatological verification and religious experience in general, however, I believe we have found that it fails as a means of approaching these issues. For Hick has produced a philosophical theology that rests upon conventions that seem to exclude the possibility of his own theological enterprise.

NOTES

[1] Two important issues arise at this point. First, as mentioned in note 58 of chapter IV, there are many philosophers in the analytic tradition who do not think that Hick can specify coherently what would constitute eschatological verification of theistic claims. For a list of publications in which Hick is opposed in this respect, see his article, "Eschatological Verification Reconsidered," *Religious Studies,* Vol. 13, No. 2 (June, 1977), p. 191. The second issue is that Hick's position depends upon the analytic tradition. Were the conventions of this tradition significantly altered, much of Hick's conceptual edifice could be jeopardized. Some of those who look for the demise of the analytic tradition are found in note 1 of chapter III.

[2] John Hick, "On Conflicting Religious Truth Claims," *Religious Studies,* Vol. 19, No. 4 (1983), p. 490.

³Ibid., pp. 490-491.

⁴Ibid., p. 487.

⁵John Hick, *Evil and the God of Love* (San Francisco: Harper and Row, Publishers, 1978), p. 13. Hick's use of evidentualist requirements is again well illustrated by his discussion of mind/body dualism. He argues that a person's consciousness or mental activity can be correlated with his or her brain activity, yet that "...we need further evidence for the identity of the thought with its brain correlate. And not only is there no such evidence, but it seems impossible to conceive what such evidence might consist of." *Death and Eternal Life* (San Francisco: Harper and Row, Publishers, 1976), p. 115. His evidentualist requirements are also always to some degree imposed when he deals with the Christian doctrines of the incarnation and the resurrection of Christ, and similar uses of evidentualism can be found in most of Hick's work, especially *Arguments for the Existence of God* (New York: The Seabury Press, 1971). His concern for evidence is much less restrictive, however, with respect to his global theology.

⁶Ninian Smart, *Beyond Ideology, Religion and the Future of Western Civilization* (New York: Harper and Row, Publishers, 1981). Wilfred Cantwell Smith, *Towards a World Theology* (Philadelphia: The Westminster Press, 1981). For a bibliography and survey of such well-known attempts to formulate a pluralist theology of world religions, see Alan Race, *Christians and Religious Pluralism: Patterns in the Christian Theology of Religions* (Maryknoll: Orbis Books, 1983).

⁷Dewi Arwell Hughes, "Christianity and Other Religions: A Review of Some Recent Discussion," *Themelios*, Vol. 9, No. 2 (1984).

⁸Wilfred Cantwell Smith, *Towards a World Theology* (Philadelphia: The Westminster Press, 1980), p. 189.

⁹John Hick, *God and the Universe of Faiths* (London: The Macmillan Press, 1973), pp. 95, 114.

¹⁰See pages 3-5 and 12 above.

¹¹See for example note 1 of chapter III here, especially Paul K. Feyerabend, *Against Method* (London: Verso, 1975).

¹²Richard Swinburne, *An Introduction to Confirmation Theory* (London: Methuen, 1973).

¹³Alvin Plantinga, "Advice to Christian Philosophers," (unpublished paper presented at Fuller Theological Seminary, February 25, 1983), p. 9.

¹⁴This example of Jones was cited in note 10 of chapter II here. It is taken from *The Sciences and the Humanities, Conflict and Reconciliation* (Berkeley: University of California Press, 1965). Its context is the section dealing with foreground/background structures on pp. 26-106. Though this book was written after he published *The Romantic Syndrome: Toward a New Method in Cultural Anthropology and History of Ideas* (Nijhof: The Hague, 1961), it can be seen as a philosophical defense of this earlier book, reprinted in 1975, which as its title suggests, is meant to provide conceptual indices for the study of culture. Though he has had this concern for cultural studies throughout much of his intellectual career, he did not often write about it until

after he produced *A History of Western Philosophy* (New York: Harcourt, Brace, 1952), which was later published in four volumes and is now in five. His studies typically continue along the lines of his theses in *The Sciences and the Humanities* and *The Romantic Syndrome* in two general respects, one quantitative, in that it is an attempted empirical investigation of the presuppositions underlying differences of opinion over the same body of data, the other nonquantitative in that it does not involve the testing of subjects. To my knowledge, he has not published the material involving the former; he takes the latter approach in his publications to date. See for instance "Philosophical Disagreements and World Views," *Proceedings and Addresses of the American Philosophical Association*, Vol. 43 (1969-70), pp.24-42; "World Views: Their Nature and Their Function," *Current Anthropology*, Vol. 13, No. 1 (1972); "*Somnio Ergo Sum:* Descartes' Three Demands," *Philosophical Literature*, Vol. 4 (1980), pp.145-166; "Julian Jaynes and the Bicameral Mind: A Case Study in the Sociology of Belief," *Philosophy and the Social Sciences*, Vol. 12 (1982), pp. 153-171. Jones' quantitative studies are more recent and I believe yet unpublished. These include the papers coauthored with William Faust, Margaret Faust, and Molly Mason Jones, entitled "Some Implicit Presuppositions of Typical Writings in the field of American Intellectual History" (1980), "Some Implicit Presuppositions Involved in the Disagreement Over the DNA Guidelines," (1980), "Paintings and Their Implicit Presuppositions: A Preliminary Report" (1981), "Paintings and Their Implicit Presuppositions: High Renaissance and Mannerism" (1982). Respectively, the first two of these are Social Science Working Papers 355 and 354, and the second two are Humanities Working Papers 66 and 75, California Institute of Technology, Pasadena, California. Although Jones' work over the last several years can be seen to stem from the two books mentioned above, he may himself have reservations with regard to some of his earlier views. For example, much has been done in linguistics that these works do not take into account. But insofar as he provides a means to compare world views, his work may be quite valuable for looking at the relationship between secular and religious points of view. This is not to say that Jones lends any credence to religion. Those interested in the plausibility of the sort of Christian view with which this essay is concerned will find A. Plantinga and N. Wolterstorff, eds., *Faith and Rationality* (Notre Dame: University of Notre Dame Press, 1983) much more pertinent than Jones. For similar apologetic texts, see note 2 of chapter II.

[16] Ibid., p. 56-57.
[17] Ibid., p. 66.
[18] Ibid., p. 61.
[19] Ibid., p. 65.
[20] Ibid., p. 69.
[21] Arthur C. McGill, "Recent Discussions of Anselm's Argument," in *The Many-Faced Argument*, ed. by John Hick and Arthur C. McGill (New York: The Macmillan Company, 1967), pp. 33-110.

[22]Anselm, *Proslogium*, trans. by S. N. Deane (Chicago: The Open Court Publishing Co., 1903), p. 11.

[23]Anselm, *Concerning Truth*, trans. by Jasper Hopkins (New York: Harper and Row, Publishers, 1967), p. 108.

[24]Anselm, *Proslogium*, trans. by Deane, pp. 21-22.

[25]For example, see Hick's criticism of Anselm in *Arguments for the Existence of God*, p. 83.

BIBLIOGRAPHY OF THE WORKS OF JOHN HICK

Books (In Chronological Order)

Hick, John H. *Faith and Knowledge*. Ithaca, N.Y.: Cornell University Press, 1957.

____. *Philosophy of Religion*. Englewood Cliffs, N.J.: Prentice-Hall, Inc., 1963.

____. ed. *Faith and the Philosophers*. New York: St. Martin's Press, 1964.

____. *Classical and Contemporary Readings in the Philosophy of Religion*. Englewood Cliffs, N.J.: Prentice-Hall, Inc., 1964.

____. ed. *The Existence of God*. New York: The Macmillan Company, 1964.

____. *Evil and the God of Love*. San Francisco: Harper & Row, Publishers, 1966.

____. Arthur C. McGill, eds. *The Many-faced Argument*. New York: The Macmillan Company, 1967.

____. *Christianity at the Centre*. New York: Herder & Herder, 1968.

____. *Arguments for the Existence of God*. New York: The Seabury Press, 1971.

____. *Biology and the Soul*. Cambridge: University Press, 1972.

____. *God and the Universe of Faiths*. London: The Macmillan Press, 1973.

____. ed. *Truth and Dialogue*. London: Sheldon Press, 1974.

____. *Death and Eternal Life*. New York: Harper & Row, Publishers, 1976.

____. ed. *The Myth of God Incarnate*. Philadelphia: Westminster Press, 1977.

____. *God Has Many Names*. London: The Macmillan Press, 1980.

____. Brian Hebblethwaite, eds. *Christianity and Other Religions*. Glasgow: William Collins Sons, 1980.

Selected Articles (In Chronological Order)

Hick, John H. "Theology and Verification." *Theology Today*, Vol. 17, No. 1 (January, 1960), 12-31.
____. "God as Necessary Being." *The Journal of Philosophy*, Vol. 57, Nos. 22 and 23 (November, 1961), 725-734.
____. "Meaning and Truth in Theology." *Religious Experience and Truth*. Edited by Sidney Hook. New York: New York University Press, 1961.
____. "Necessary Being." *Scottish Journal of Theology*, Vol. 14, No. 4 (December, 1961), 353-369.
____. "A Plea for Systematic Theology." *Regina* (The Magazine of the Queen's College, Birmingham), No. 3 (1969), 15-17.
____. "A New Form of Theistic Argument." *Proceedings of the XIVth International Congress of Philosophy*, Vienna, Vol. V (1970), 336-341.
____. "The Reconstruction of Christian Belief for Today and Tomorrow: I." *Theology*, Vol. 73, No. 602 (August, 1970), 339-345.
____. "The Reconstruction of Christian Belief for Today and Tomorrow: II." *Theology*, Vol. 73, No. 603 (September, 1970), 399-405.
____. "Freedom and the Irenaean Theodicy Again." *The Journal of Theological Studies*, Vol. 21, Part 2 (October, 1970), 419-422.
____. "Faith, Evidence, Coercion Again." *Australasian Journal of Philosophy*, Vol. 49, No. 1 (May, 1971), 78-81.
____. "Reincarnation: A Critical Examination of One Form of Reincarnation Theory." *The Journal of Religious Studies*, Vol. III, No. 1 (1971), 56-69.
____. "The Christian View of Other Faiths." *The Expository Times*, Vol. 84, No. 2 (November, 1972), 36-39.
____. "Coherence and the God of Love Again." *Journal of Theological Studies*, Vol. 24, Part 2 (October, 1973),

522-528.

_____. "Mystical Experience as Cognition." *Mystics and Scholars*. Edited by Harold Coward and Terence Penelhum. Waterloo, Canada: Wilfred Laurier University Press, 1977.

_____. "Eschatological Verification Reconsidered." *Religious Studies*, Vol. 13, No. 2 (June, 1977), 189-202.

_____. "Towards A Philosophy of Religious Pluralism." *Neue Zeitschrift fur systematische Theologie*, Vol. 11, No. 2 (1980), 131-149.

_____. "On Grading Religions." *Religious Studies*, Vol. 17, No. 4 (1981), 451-467.

_____. "On Conflicting Religious Truth Claims." *Religious Studies*, Vol. 19, No. 4 (1983), 485-491.

INDEX

Hell, 15
Hick, John, 1, 20f
Hinduism, 107
Humanism, 17, 28
Hume, David, 59f, 72

Idealism, 22
Incarnation, 15, 119
Input-alignment, 122
Interpretation, 8, 84, 89

James, 85
Jeremiah, 8, 83, 106
Jesus Christ, 16, 62, 83, 106, 119
Jastrow's duck-rabbit, 49, 79
Job, 85
Jones, W.T., 29ff, 120

Kant, Immanuel, 6f, 22, 52
Kaufmann, E., 58
Knowledge, 75f
Koran, 5, 89

Language,
  cognitive, 3, 27, 28ff, 45
  nature of, 9, 29ff
  noncognitive, 4f, 27, 28ff, 36
Lewis, C.S., 92
Linguistic continuum, 30
Logical positivism, 9ff, 23

Macbeth, 42
Mackie, J.L., 66
Martians, 110
Mavrodes, George, 27, 37f, 93, 121ff
Meaning, 46ff
Mermaids, 47, 90, 111
Miller, C. C., 58
Muhammad, 5

Natural theology, 40, 43
Naturalism, 8, 17, 72, 118ff
Newton, I., 21, 55

Pain, 9, 49, 69, 78, 89
Pancosmic consciousness, 73
Parable of travelers, 61f
Perception, 102f, 121, 123
Perceptual field, 30
Phenomenalism, 50, 74
Phillips, D. Z., 41
Pilate, Pontius, 106
Plantinga, Alvin, 27, 37, 93, 120
Prediction, 12f
Principle of plentitude, 111, 117
Probability, 69f, 91
Ptolemaic scheme, 121
Pyramid power, 110

Rational doubt, 12, 59, 78
Relativism, 45, 56, 77
Religious experience, 78, 80ff, 90, 98ff, 123
Revelation, 62, 84, 86, 89
Rowe, William, 92

Salvation, 19, 88f
Schleiermacher, F., 24
Science and religion, 15, 17, 73, 118f
Scripture, 62, 84, 86, 89
Seeing-as, 79
Shiva, 7
Significance, 8, 52ff, 79ff
Sikhism, 89
Smart, Ninian, 117, 127
Smith, W.C., 117, 127
Solipsism, 96ff
Soul making, 19f, 79
Suffering, 9, 18, 49, 51, 59, 69, 78, 86, 89
Swinburne, Richard, 23, 65, 76f

Synthetic statement, 10

Taylor, Richard, 75
Telepathy, 66
Tennant, C.R., 65, 70, 74f, 76f,
   90
Theism, 8, 55, 72, 118ff
Theodicy, 18, 77ff
Theology,
   global, 2, 22, 63, 88
   natural, 40, 60
   process, 40, 60
Thiselton, A., 41
Tibetan Book of the Dead, 24
Total interpretation, 71f, 74
Truth, 21, 32, 35, 75f, 83

Unicorns, 111
Universal salvation, 19, 88f
Upanishads, 89

Vedas, 89
Verifiability 5, 47
Verification 9, 11, 23, 39, 56ff
Vishnu, 7

Whitehead, A.N., 40, 60, 67
Wittgenstein, L., 27, 49, 79
Wolterstorff, N., 41, 44
World,
   religions, 22, 63, 88
   ambigious nature of, 8, 48f,
      54, 81

Zuurdeeg, W., 41